The News Inside

The News Inside

Poems

Bill Brown

Iris Press
Oak Ridge, Tennessee

Copyright © 2010 by Bill Brown

All rights reserved. No portion of this book may be reproduced in any form or by any means, including electronic storage and retrieval systems, without explicit, prior written permission of the publisher, except for brief passages excerpted for review and critical purposes.

Cover Photograph, "Cypress Reflections on a Foggy Morning"
Copyright © 2010 by Tina Marie Brookes

Iris Press is an imprint of the Iris Publishing Group, Inc.
www.irisbooks.com

Design by Robert B. Cumming, Jr.

Library of Congress Cataloging-in-Publication Data

Brown, Bill, 1948 Sept. 17-
  The news inside : poems / by Bill Brown.
     p. cm.
  ISBN 978-1-60454-210-3 (pbk. : alk. paper)
  I. Title.
  PS3552.R68523N48 2010
  811'.54—dc22
                                            2010024948

Acknowledgments

Thanks to the following publications in which these poems first appeared:

A Dream In The Clouds (Anthology from BoBo Strategies, Chicago): "Learning, West Tennessee, 1962"
Alca-lines (NCTE Appalachian Journal): "The Varsity Sweater"
Appalachian Heritage: "Ants"
Appalachian Journal: "Cold Comfort," "On a Train Near Shining Rock"
Asheville Poetry Review: "The Graciousness of Soil"
Atlanta Review: "Journey," "Myotis Lucifugus"
Aurorean: "The Appointment"
Big Muddy: "Raccoon," "Tonight Alone"
Borderlands (The Texas Poetry Review): "The Melting"
Clinch Mountain Review: "Hip Surgery," "Pan," "Stasis," "Subtext"
Cold Mountain Review: "Dark Fire"
Connecticut Review: "Dejection in February," "Pruning," "Wednesday Miracles"
Crab Creek Review: "Driving the Country Roads on Sunday"
Crow (The Tennessee Literary Project Online Anthology): "Lake County, West Tennessee"
Eclipse: "Apologies," "The Little Blue Corporal," "This Poem"
English Journal: "Breaking Sod," "Frame," "Love Poem"
Icon: "Midnight Mass"
Into the Teeth of the Wind: "Waking"
Mainstreet Rag: "My Brother's Crow," "Winter Solstice, Random Thoughts"
Maypop (Tennessee Writer's Alliance Online Journal): "The Light"
Motif (Anthology from Mote Books on Music): "My Niece and I Listen to Jazz"

Motif (Anthology from Mote Books on Chance): "Listening to Japanese Music at Starbucks, I Think of Basho"
Nashville Arts Magazine: "What the Wind Says"
Number One: "Counting Stars," "Crocker Springs," "One for Elkin," "Planting Iris," "The End of the World, 1956," "Whisper"
Outscapes (Anthology from Knoxville Writer's Guild): "Landscape Meditation"
Phantasmagoria: "The Prayerful Agnostic"
POEM: "May Morning, Reelfoot Lake," "Silos," "Talking to Dust," "The Stain"
Poems and Plays: "The Calling"
Rhino: "Coyotes, Lake County, Colorado"
Slant: "In the Orthopedic Clinic," "Solomon's Ants (as 'Ants')," "The Knife in the Kitchen Drawer," "Weeding"
Southern Poetry Review: "November Poem"
Tar River Poetry: "Long Division"
Tennessee English Journal: "Chanukah, West Tennessee, 1964," "Soft Mornings"
Visions International: "Siasconset Time"
White Pelican Review: "Names of Creeks"

"Siasconset Time" is anthologized in *Nantucket Poems* and in *Proposing on the Brooklyn Bridge: Poems about Marriage,* Poetworks, Grayson Press.

"Waking" is anthologized in *75 Poems on Retirement,* University of Iowa Press.

Several of these poems appeared in the chapbook, *Yesterday's Hay,* published by Pudding House Press in 2006.

My deepest thanks to Larry Richman whose editing skills and friendship have made this book possible. He is my syntax guru.

Jeff Hardin, friend and fellow poet, inspired me to write daily, and in doing so, helped me reclaim my silence and my voice in a loud year.

I thank Bob Cumming, whose wise advice helped me shape the final version of this book.

I thank J.J. Street and Beto Cumming for teaching a man born in the wrong century how to use his new computer.

I thank my colleagues and students at Vanderbilt University for inspiration and support.

Bread Loaf School of English, Middlebury College, and Radford University, your influence and heart are still with me two decades out.

I greatly appreciate Humanities Tennessee, The Tennessee Arts Commission and the Downtown Nashville Public Library for continuing to support the written and spoken word.

To my brothers and sister for celebrating my myth-making and fictive retellings of our family's life—bless each of you.

And most of all, I thank my wife, Suzanne, for being my truest and best reader, on the page and off.

—Bill Brown

CONTENTS

The News Inside   13

I   COUNTING

The Melting   17
Dark Fire   18
One for Elkin   19
Silos   20
Pronoun   21
Counting Stars   22
Stasis   23
The Knife in the Kitchen Drawer   24
Love Poem   25
November Poem   26
Fragile   27
Winter Solstice, Random Thoughts   28
Bookish   29
Dejection in February   31
Names   32
Pan   34
The Stain   35
Soft Mornings   36
The List   38
Listening to Japanese Music at Starbucks, I Think of Basho   40

II   BACK WHEN

Breaking Sod   43
The End of the World, 1956   44
Black Widow   45
West Tennessee, Small Town 50's Farewell   46
Myotis Lucifugus   47
Ants   48
Learning, West Tennessee, 1962   49

My Brother's Crow   50
Chanukah, West Tennessee, 1964   52
Hometown Apocalyptic, 1965   53
Shotgun   55
Razing Hell   57
Back When   59
The Four Second Rule   61
Lake County, West Tennessee   63
The Varsity Sweater   64
Landscape Meditation   65
Tonight, Alone   66

III   THE DANCE

The Dance   69
Long Division   70
Wednesday Miracles   71
Raccoon   73
To the Dead Opossum on the Roadside   75
The Little Blue Corporal   76
Coyotes, Lake County, Colorado   77
Solomon's Ants   79
Symbolism   81
The Short List   82
The Light   83
Pragmatic Angel   84
The Stolen Day   85
Lullaby   86
The Living   87
Watering the Herbs   89
Frame   90
The Ten Most Violent Cities   91
Today   92

IV The Calling

This Poem 95
What the Wind Says 97
The Calling 99
Two Unanswered Questions 100
Tapping 101
Gravid 103
Heart 104
In the Orthopedic Clinic 105
Hip Surgery 107
My Niece and I Listen to Jazz 108
Subtext 109
Planting Iris 110
Weeding 111
Talking to Dust 112
Pushing the Sky 114
Descent 115
Ascent 116
Crocker Springs 117
Driving Ridge Road, Writing This Poem 118
Whisper 120
Autumn Thoughts 122

V Waking

Waking 125
The Appointment 126
Thespian 127
The Names of Creeks 129
May Morning, Reelfoot Lake 130
Siasconset Time 131
Early this Moring 132
On a Trail Near Shining Rock 133
Lifting 134
Cold Comfort 136

Midnight Mass   138
Pruning   139
Alchemy   140
Driving Country Roads on Sunday   142
The Prayerful Agnostic   143
Apologies   144
August Moon   146
Druid Thoughts in November   147
Journey   149
The Graciousness of Soil   151
Indigo   153

VI CODA

Solstice   157

The News Inside

The news we hear is full of grief for that future,
but the real news inside here
is there's no news at all.
—Rumi

        Rumi, the headline news
this morning is not new—a gunman enters a
fitness center and opens fire on an aerobics class
killing four.
        Surely someone should report
that a charitable person in every American city fed
breakfast to a homeless family.
        On my creek walk this morning
an eastern kingbird eating a late summer hatch
says the bugs are tasty.
        Early August rains inspire
the mock orange to bloom again, perfuming the nest
where the wrens have hatched their second brood.
        Those apples grow from the Gift,
and sink back into the Gift, you said. Rumi, what is
the *reedsong* in one heart worth?
        I swear I heard it this morning
in the sift of cottonwood leaves on Sulfur Fork, or in
my breath, or both.
        Tell me, who owns *that future,*
Old Sufi Mystic, knocking on both sides of the door?

I

COUNTING

The Melting

There should be hope in the leaves' first turning—
summer green fringed gold and crimson, webbed
hands reaching out against the curtain's blue.

Winter and what it takes from the heart
is almost worth it. Year by blessed year,
in the shortened days, something is stolen

that cannot be reclaimed—a swelling in the chest
when night comes soon. At a certain age
a man takes a season's beginnings, the small

beauties—frozen rings on creek rocks,
the first skein of ice in the horse trough.
He holds it to the morning sun and it burns

his palm as it drips through his fingers.
Each year he grips it tighter
to see his face melt in the fire.

Dark Fire

Driving down Walker Creek Road,
I carry the memory of a younger self
who admired the deep wooded hollow
and the gray tobacco barns. In early autumn,

Dark-fire smoke drafted through roof vents
perfuming an October sky. It's New Year's
and my father's memory curls in the bark
of yellow birch along the creek.

A neighbor's horses drink from a trough.
Water riddling from their big lips
catches the sun. Today, I notice
the names of roads anew—

Kelly Willis Road, Glenne Lea, Baker Station.
What's become of people who wore those names?
I marvel at how place is marked by names
whose memories have long since faded,

locked in some county vault filled
with unread records. I can't imagine
a road named Bill Brown.
I'd rather have my countenance

thought of as I think of my father
among the birches. Let my name
fade away with the lips of those who speak it
like the dark-fire smoke rising in fall.

One for Elkin

> *You can lose yourself, you can find yourself,*
> *On the stretching plains of October.*
> —Holly and Elkin Brown

Elkin, it's nearing October's end
and I'm driving in the rain
listening to your CD, watching
leaves palm the country road—
and I think of your fingers
teasing the Celtic heart from a song.
When I first met you, I thought
this man is a self, a humble self,
with a keen wit and an easy smile.
Too bad the meek can't inherit the earth
as the Bible states. But according
to Thoreau, a man can own all that
he observes. So this morning,
I'll own the Highland Ridge,
Sulfur Fork Creek and the rouge
of sumac and sassafras painting
the roadside. You sang of October,
the month of your passing,
in a voice like Dylan's, not pretty
but real. And I meet you again
through your music, and remember
how you stared at a painting
of an African child in my living room.
Your eyes welled to the brim,
and you said that a refugee painted it.
I wanted to ask how you knew.
Today I hear your answer
in the thorny truth of the song.
Elkin, Joni Mitchell sang,
We are stardust, we are fallen.
This morning, I claim the landscape
for you—the one you have joined.

Silos

—for R. N.

This morning I see an old grain bin
and think of a gifted painter,
our studios adjacent at an art colony.
Richard gained prominence painting silos.
When he returned from Vietnam,
he painted from California home to West Virginia.
I saw him one morning sanding a beautiful image
from a canvas he had worked on for days.
Half joking, I said *you could have given it to me.*
Without looking up, he said that he couldn't live
knowing it was wrong. For days I worked
with that idea. I remembered my mother saying
the product was in the making. I thought
of Van Gogh, who bore heavy equipment
on his back to suffer for art, and Beethoven,
deaf and ill, directing his Ninth Symphony
for the first time. At the finale, he had to be
turned around by a musician to see the audience's
resounding ovation. Now I know, Richard's
was a patient, studied journey, state by state
to put the war behind. He searched for those
grounded missiles, the most beautiful made
of old brick or stone. And when he reached
the West Virginia border, perhaps he dreamed
the perfect silo armed with grain,
crumbling earthward, aimed at nothing.

Pronoun

You are thankful this morning for *it,*
the pronoun of existence. It was first light.
It was the song of the towhee.

It was your wife dreaming in the next room.
It finally felt like spring. It smelled like rich coffee
brewing on the stove. It reminded you

of your mother's kitchen, the scent of fresh bread
on baking day. It was over when the doctor
took his thumbs and closed your father's eyes.

It was the last time your mother stood at the window
and watched maple shadows burnish the porch.
It was the call celebrating a grandniece born in May.

It comes like memory, it comes as evening
edges the garden and makes you watchful
of storms, makes you glimpse the "It"

of the first time you recognized your adult
loneliness, unnamable and undividable from
the stranger of the self. Perhaps it's in cahoots

with the God particle the collider hasn't found.
Like the warmth of your cat sleeping at your feet,
you feel it in your shoulders when your wife stands

behind you. It will one day get you, but it has given
you this—the towhee's song at first light,
your lover dreaming in another room.

Counting Stars

On a dark cliff, a Joshua tree claws the sky
like the prophet pointing toward the city of Ai,
or a grand conductor, baton in hand.

A man rests his back against a rock
and counts desert stars. Night plays
the Ninth Symphony in his head.

He thinks of deaf Beethoven—
rumors have it, he sawed off piano legs,
placed the instrument on the floor,

to feel music vibrate beneath his chest.
The man slows his breath to stop
the spheres from racing. He presses

his chest against the sand to feel
the day's heat rise toward the sky.
In the dark arroyo, an owl calls,

a coyote yips at a moon sliver.
A shimmering silence leaches
the day's warmth from the air.

For a moment he hears his dead
whispering over his left shoulder.
What are they saying?

He counts on as East Mountain
begins to glow, and the morning star
is lost to morning.

Stasis

—for Suzanne

Sometimes the way you stare
at your art, your mouth twisting
into a puzzle, your eyes darker green

than when you daydream, I want
to know where you go to find
the images that shape a dark

figure by a window, the curtain
hanging blue, the light filtered
by winter trees. Why place a feather,

golden-teared, beside the frame?
Why make your palette from handmade
paper—snakeskin, hornet's nest,

old stationery left in an attic—
fibers lost or shed? Winter evenings
when willow's spring green is but

a preponderance in dark limbs,
I watch you stare at the skylight
high on the wall, and for a moment,

I think you see the shadowed stranger
in your painting welcome night, as she must,
ready to turn from the window but frozen.

The Knife in the Kitchen Drawer

My wife took the knife away
from a parent at school who told
her solemnly that her daughter
was in cahoots with Satan.

He stalked her day and night,
hid behind the shower curtain
to keep her from washing, slept
with her child while she slept,

watched through her mirror
and made her decorate her face
like a clown. After two hours
on the phone with Protective Services

and The Crisis Center, the police
came, cuffed her and took her
to Central State. I sharpen the knife
on a whetstone my father used

to hone his Barlow, and put it back
in the drawer by itself, covered
with the imagined blood of voices, voices—
and devils and a child of four

now in foster care. Corroded
with my wife's nightmares, it shines
like polished silver, its blade sharp.
It will never be used. It will never come clean.

Love Poem

You snore like my father, and you can cook
nothing. The kitchen is mine. Isn't it perfect—

we've lived 38 years with a broken dishwasher,
the storage place for crumpled foil containers

we scrub and promise to reuse. What is it
about evenings with nothing to do but sip

wine on the porch and listen to our neighbor's
peacocks shock the moon and the geldings

whinny in the wind which is always present
like stars, that even on cloudy nights,

we know are there? How perfectly beautiful—
your green eyes flash at an injustice, so like

my grandmother's whose quick glance would
scare a lie. Even at our age desire whispers

and our eager hands know each other. Still,
your curls snooze on the pillow like a girl's.

November Poem

November shook my name
    like wind in orchard limbs,
        then lost it among a scatter of leaves.

And despite the inconvenience,
    I have nothing to sign today,
        just a self among anonymous trees.

And what does it matter
    if lichen can't be translated,
        or limestone fossils go unarchived

along the roads that link our towns?
    And the proof we leave of living?
        Too much to contemplate on a nameless day

when sorrow is filed in November blue
    because loss mailed a letter without a stamp.
        It will find its way here soon.

Fragile

Night can hide a person's name,
lose it in dream's sensual closet
or coal bin, thick with soot,
stenciled with the tracks of rats.
Once camping alone
on Roan High Bald,
a storm flapping the little tent—
I became a bird soaring
darkness over stony leaps.
Awakened by a racing pulse,
I called out my name
and nothing answered,
but a thunder clap
and the earthy smell of rain.
Today, the morning window
opens my eyes, my name
tarnished but still intact.
Night's memory, tattered
with the strips of different selves,
the unnamed ghosts we carry
with us, some strangers,
others vague but familiar,
the conversations we share
with them, faces escaped,
activated in the electric
blood, that pliant gallery.
A whippoorwill call,
a train whistle, a lonesome
sound invites them in,
drags the cargo of the self
along tracks, rushing
toward a nameless town.

Winter Solstice, Random Thoughts

The sign on the Ridgetop Diner reads
Pray for our troops / two ham biscuits 99 cents.
The Gideon Baptist Church sign reads
This is not a hotel for saints, but a refuge for sinners.

If I had any sense, I'd pack my bag and move in—
but I doubt they'd have me. Even a band
of Jehovah's Witnesses dropped smiling pamphlets
on the porch and left without knocking.

Eleven degrees, four days before Christmas
and nothing's worth saving. The bearded cedars
and scraggly pines the only green. Winter hills
brush gray with hardwoods. The resident circle

of buzzards overhead, hardly any traffic
except a scrawny coyote dancing the road for food.
I'm hunting too—there's a universe here,
my kitchen table and all the places I miss—

the Middle Fork of the Salmon, Shining Rock,
Bread Loaf Mountain, Ocracoke, Tellico Plains,
Reelfoot Lake. *Sweet Jesus,* My dead mother
would say, *60 years old and still whining.*

Longing, Mother, still longing.
I stare at a photo my wife made years ago—
a simple pier built between two cypress trees.
Lake water and wind have carved ice sculpture.

The walkway from shore has long since fallen.
Restless eagles wait for the fog to lift.
A lone rocker stares into a winter whiteout,
and there's no one left to sit there.

Bookish

The books on the nightstand tire of being
added to when they've hardly been
touched, their pages crisp and unmarked,

their stories imprisoned, sentenced to be unlived.
In desperation they read my dreams instead—
the story of a boy whose character is never

quite developed, unable to make decisions,
uncomfortable in his own skin, obsessed
with the circumstances of his father's death—

Shakespeare did it better, they think.
And how desperately he adored his mother,
left alone with her during adolescence. Sounds

Oedipal, the book on Jung comments. It's all
been done before they agree, magical realism
with rabbit tricks: lazy student experiments

with drugs, becomes a poet, then a teacher,
how unoriginal, he must be impressed with
the Beats—I bet he's never been to San Francisco.

Sometimes their outrage wakes me. I tell my wife
to turn over and stop snoring. Other times I find them
rearranged, Stevens separated from Hemingway

to avoid a fistfight at Key West, Joyce and Marquez
in a jealous feud over narration. Several times my
water glass has been knocked off the table.

Tonight I turn in early, thumb through a *New Yorker*
and read the comics. I notice *The Modern Poets,* teetering:
Ginsberg howls, Plath rants about her Daddy. Thomas urges

not to go gentle into that good night, Delmore Schwartz
says The Heavy Bear That Goes With Me is restless,
Frost thinks that I've got miles to go before I sleep.

Dejection in February

Vacant thoughts empty from
the crowns of winter trees

and flavor an otherwise stale sky.
Roadside crow talk, a gnat hatch

to feed warblers, and the mocking-
bird's piecemeal chant

are welcome, help heal a day
when forgotten years steer

their ragtag caravan into the drive
like prodigals. But there are no

fatted lambs to roast, just a beleaguered
old ewe that one can't bear to sacrifice.

I could make this poem concrete
if I had the courage of story.

But these misdeeds, both painful
and precious, wear loose fitting metaphors,

their shirt sleeves too long,
their weary coats moth-eaten.

On this late winter day
memory needs a vagueness tonic,

and eyes prop open
to a sun gone cold.

Names

This April morning
    I stare out the kitchen door
    and consider a world without names—
    no Carolina wrens

busy building no nest
    in no porch gourd,
    flutterless and songless.
    Goldfinch, house finch, nuthatch,

indistinguishable,
    no maple and black gum leaves
    without movement and shadow
    in no breeze.

My mother loved names—
    from my earliest age
    trees became oak,
    sassafras and beech.

Childhood friends, Barbara, Donny
    and Linda Jo—names fresh
    on my tongue, faces still bright
    in memory's storied play,

their plight lost some forty years.
    How simple to live vague,
    like's job made easier—nothing
    tastes like salt, like honey, like gall.

Since there would be no name
    for life, death would be anonymous,
    nameless Satan would drift in limbo
    without an ego.

And God, whom many religions
   honor by not naming—
   the great "I am,"
   or just a pregnant pause—

perhaps any part of speech would do.
   On second thought, I'll let Adam
   keep his most productive job,
   and leave Eve an apple to taste.

This morning, winter forgotten,
   I accept the curse of names
   and its fretted aftermath. Wrens
   build nests in Amish gourds,

and my mother's grave
   can't erase
   the names of trees
   she gave to me.

Pan

One horn gnawed off,
the other jutting from the skull
like a lopsided unicorn's,
a goat head deposited
in my spring garden by dogs
leans its exhausted chin
against a stone, purple hyacinths
reflecting in glazed eyes.
I could stick it on a broom handle,
circle it with my wife's old slip
and finally give Gertrude Smudge,
across the road, evidence enough
to call the sheriff about my pagan ways.

Instead, I honor this tired Pan
by burying his head beneath
a mound of seed potatoes,
and in July, when tender lumps
grow round and firm against
the mother root, I'll harvest them,
and carry them as a gift
to Mrs. Smudge,
first new potatoes,
food for the gods.

The Stain

To stare at nothing is to learn by heart
What all of us will be swept into
—Mark Strand

The stain remains on sunny days
like a life that thrives on sorrow,
a reoccurring dream that sleep
knows by heart—when sleep

becomes the closet you can't open—
no hands attached to your wrists,
no doorknob to turn— just
a night window that mirrors

the inside; even passing car lights
won't circle the ceiling edge—
the news is stacked with bodies,
the ribs of starving children,

American Idol, and a luxury cruise
run aground. In this world it takes
courage to hope—darkness, that sad
pilgrimage, is a coward's journey.

Soft Mornings

Morning opens like an old book
      I know by heart—
         silver lines wet maple leaves,

goldfinches speak to cone flowers,
      and a memory of childhood
      left over from sleep—

a boy watches his mother prune roses,
      checks fallen apricots for worms,
      separates each half from the seed

and eats in the tree's shade.
      Fifty years ago and the sweetness
      still lingers on my lips.

Today's heat will hit the nineties,
      and an unspoken prayer for rain
      gathers outside the market

in farmers' eyes. Their pickups
      wear the same dust
      creased in their broken smiles.

They smoke and kick tires,
      wait on wives who make
      small talk with the cashier.

Creek beds write clay-hardened hieroglyphics,
      an earthbound language no schooling unteaches,
      except in a mall world that worships

    the new and history is a price tag.
        Above the ridge,
           a mountain shadows low clouds.

Something like God lives there,
        holds up with bird calls and mist—
        without praying, I pray for rain.

So many metaphors wasted,
        away from corn and wheat and hay—
        nothing tied to dirt,

but a soft morning rescues the heart for a time—
        maple shadows,
        the taste of apricots,

the memory of my mother's
        strong hands
           among the thorns.

The List

No furniture inside the house.
No truck outside.
No red couch with pillows
turned to hide juice stains.
No crayon hieroglyphics
in the playroom.
Wedding pictures have abandoned
their spot above the fireplace.
No maple kitchen table
where coffee was sipped,
supper was served—
small talk, morning and night,
stories embellished,
the dead unburied,
the war buddies with Polish
names remembered.
The wounded soldier
from Guam on my father's
battleship, not a hand
on either arm, held his
coffee cup with nubs.
For three days my father
fed him in the mess hall,
wrote my mother
he'd never complain about
sore joints and a mechanic's
bruised fingers again.
The old spaniel vanished
from his porch corner.
A house emptied of voices,
the grease stain
on the kitchen wall

from a skillet fire,
the only story left.
It bled through coat
after coat of paint,
and is still bleeding.

Listening to Japanese Music at Starbucks, I Think of Basho

     How fitting, my old companion,
that while I drink iced coffee
I hear your words rise from memory.
Isn't it right that *The broom
forgets about the snow.* If it
lasts another year the broom
will know the snow again.
The spider forgets the crone
on the porch swing after she's gone,
and the wind will forget the spider once
the eggs are laid and flies are wrapped.

     You said, *Already I can see
my own wind-bleached bones.* I never
saw my bones, Basho, but I dreamed
my ashes dusting a mountainside,
or the decaying of flesh, a type
of combustion, my physics teacher said.
We are all burning, our matter waiting
to shape another form.

     A cold wind cuts me,
you said. Yes, the burning gets frigid
as winters stack in the heart's storeroom.
I am cut too by your words—some things
centuries don't change and the detail
in experience means more than time.
Whatever mystery awaits, forgetfulness
and memory, like death, are stains
we can't remove.

     *Just butterflies
and sunlight,* you said,
in the whole empty meadow.

II

BACK WHEN

Breaking Sod

Uncle Roy mounted two old saddles
on the cultivator, strapped Tommy
and me in, signaled the mule to begin,

and we became rodeo hands breaking
the back of the sod. Mule manure
smelled pungent on disk tines,

rows of soil formed in front
as we bucked that bronco backwards.
Our faces smiled through masks

of sweat and mud, our muscles
jarred into spasms, our voices
hoarse from yelling. The sun

counted down the afternoon,
crows crossed above dust clouds,
buzzards wound a coil in the sky,

soil loosened its muster,
smooth enough for sowing.
Uncle Roy, dead this week

at ninety-two, Tommy and me
too old and soft for plowing,
the sun still counting.

The End of the World, 1956

On Friday nights, my sister and I
hid in our uncle's fallout shelter.
Aunt Elise listened to baseball while
our parents and brother watched *Dragnet*.
We played at domestic affairs,

locked away from the world, not
knowing if our grandparents survived
the first minute or were doomed
to the slow decay of cells. We dusted
and straightened the cans—beans,

beef stew, chicken noodle soup.
We wrote letters to the dying,
we prayed to Jesus—our memoirs
stashed for aliens who would one day
land on earth and grieve for the violence

of leaders who condemned the meek
to oblivion. When it was time
to go home to our unsafe house
devoid of bomb shelter or TV,
our father sneaked down to observe

our histrionics, and winking
at my brother, whispered—
*kneel under the table, put
your head between your legs,
and kiss your sweet ass goodbye.*

Black Widow

Some things you're not supposed to own.
I found her at Grandmother's house
under a rock, black pump body
and crab-like legs, her red hourglass
keeping time. I coaxed her into
a Mason jar, added grass, and hid
her in a pouch. My brother's book
said that she held death in her fangs.
I could shake her if I wanted. Don't
pretend that you've never desired
to possess a certain danger,
harbor your prize from others,
take it from its vault and jiggle it,
some control of what we inherit at birth
(hourglass and fat darkness).
I've heard of soldiers who smuggle
live grenades, bayonets, human ears,
and keep them hidden in attic boxes
until they die, leaving their shrapnel
for others to find. I carried the hidden jar,
and when I dropped and broke it in town,
my father saw the spider and shook
his head. He took it on a newspaper
into the alley and let it live
as I scooped up the glass.
My father was a simple, gentle man
with like solutions. "Be careful what
you hide and play with," he said.

West Tennessee, Small Town 50's Farewell

Summers grew oppressive, mosquitoes summoned
from surrounding rivers, Forked Deer, Obion,
Mississippi, swamped our little town.

The mosquito truck combed neighborhoods
early evening— cloud of insecticide as thick
as racism following like a scorpion tail.

We played kick-the-can and king-on-the-hill,
dressed as Roy Rogers or Davy Crocket,
we knocked off Japs and Indians with our

BB guns like beer cans. Our politicians
were schooled in language manipulation. They
knew how changing one letter made rule, ruler,

spit, spite, spine, spin, morning, mourning,
hat, hate. On Sundays we dressed buttoned
down and loafered, with cotton khakis,

and madras jackets polishing the church pews
as steeples reached at heaven, where even
light's spectrum separated into its constituent colors.

Myotis Lucifugus

Second week in July and Tennessee cornfields
grow thick with green swords that fence in the wind.
A storm brewing in the Gulf has sent thunderheads
thumbing up the Mississippi and summer drought
is over for a time. Country church steeples spear the sky.
When I was a boy, I wanted to climb
into our church steeple and talk with God.
One Sunday I found the door unlocked
that hid the ladder. I worked my way up slowly,
terrified at my own curiosity. Instead of God,
I found a clapperless old bell, a smearing
of pigeon droppings and a dead bat, which
I hid in my inside coat pocket to sneak home.
I sat on the family pew next to my mother,
thinking how mortified she would be
to know that I was taking Holy Communion
with a dead bat in my pocket. I swallowed the host
and remembered that it turned into the flesh of Jesus.
To make matters worse, the sermon was on angels.
A presence in my pocket pressed against my chest,
and I felt the bat's heart beat with mine.
At home, the encyclopedia said Myotis Lucifugus—
little brown bat. In secret, I buried it
in our animal cemetery with a turtle, a rabbit,
and two dogs. I spread its wings one last time
and asked God to accept the steeple bat.
Fifty years later and I'm still talking to God,
usually when I'm driving alone looking
in the rear view mirror as if He were a child
in the back seat counting red barns.
Today I know that *Lucifugus* comes from Latin—
shunning the light. I think of the bat asleep
in the steeple that pointed toward heaven,
when all along paradise was flying in darkness
over the Forked Deer River, a gut full
of mosquitoes, a gift of summer rain.

Ants

I was thirteen and on a trip with my preacher's
family to hold a revival in East Kentucky.
One morning we woke early to drive for breakfast
in a deep hollow far from town. At the end
of a crooked road, a brace of mountain curs,
ribs sculpting the sides of their chests, snarled
at our car as we pulled beside the cabin.

The dogs slinked beneath the porch as
a weathered man in overalls welcomed us.
His arms balanced a child as wary as the curs.
His wife was flushed from cooking on a smoky stove
that smelled of kindling. The aroma of human sweat
mixed with the food: eggs, scrambled and fried,
tall scratch biscuits, milk gravy, and country bacon
spotted with the crisp exoskeletons of ants
like the forgotten husks of cicadas.

The prayer offered, heaping plates were
passed around. I knew without looking,
that Reverend Beard trained his eyes on me,
not because God would punish the squeamish stomach
of a town boy, but because of the pride it took
a poor family to offer a week's table at a sitting.

I'm not certain why we never spoke of the ants.
I remember crunching each one and mingling its
bitterness with the sweet flavor of smokehouse meat,
much to the interest of the little girl who stared
at me in wonder. Her green eyes held mine
as she trimmed the bugs off her bacon
and flirted with the town boy who ate ants.

Learning, West Tennessee, 1962

West Tennessee schools closed for cotton picking,
so Finley and Hog Wallow kids could drag burlap bags

behind them like bad memories—stuffed with middling,
sharp hulls and sweat. The September scorch burnt

white necks red and browned arms and hands.
Most pickers were *Negroes* from the bottoms,

glad to have enough work to survive part of a year.
Back in school, pigeons outside Latin class

cooed their morning prayers. Miss Kirby closed
the windows *to keep out the heat.* We simmered

in stale air and boredom. Becky Lewis sat in back,
her cheerleader skirt hiked, and I learned nothing.

Fall maples turned red. The blue sky was blank.
At first freeze we went hunting. We walked

stubbled cotton fields with pocks of mud and ice
to startle rabbits from their hiding. Talk of civil rights

sandwiched our little town. Birds of a feather, my uncle preached.
In spring pigeons outside Latin class cooed their morning prayers.

Miss Kirby closed the window *to keep out the cool.*
We simmered in stale air and boredom. Who would

guess a black man would one day be our President,
the year Becky Lewis sat in back and I learned nothing.

My Brother's Crow

Crows don't balk at epilepsy.
    They are given to raucous fits,
    flapping their wings, cursing
    existence for its tricks.

Mornings it broke the silence
    of oak shadows taunting
    his bedroom window like
    a snake charmer.

My brother raised the pane
    to see what it had stolen:
    Eisenhower dimes,
    pop-tops, carnival jewelry—

glittery amulets to ward off darkness.
    The crow bobbed its head
    in the room, leery
    of enclosure.

My brother's medicines
    sat on the bedside table:
    one to drug, two to regulate
    current in the brain.

The crow scanned the room
    for what the night had hidden:
    grinding teeth, cramping muscles,
    petty pauses between the golden

threads of wakefulness.
    Tribal people know
    that heaven marks the beautiful.
    In our little town,

my brother's fits trapped
    the chaos of stars, mapped
    empty spaces where
    a dark winged thing might go.

CHANUKAH, WEST TENNESSEE, 1964

In the Holocaust film, Nazis stormed
your home at dinner before the candle
could burn on the Menorah.
You were bound to your wheelchair
like the sacred pact Jews made
with Yahweh. But as if covenants
could be broken, they carried
your chair to the balcony to
teach you how to fly. For just
a moment you might have
spread wings like an angel
guarding the temple, but instead,
you swam against gravity, embracing
the pavement like a clumsy lover,
arms and legs limp, a child's doll
left in the street alone.

I left the movie to nurse a beer
in the lonely corner of a bar,
and remembered my boyhood pal,
Ben Stern, who got permission to attend
a camping trip during Chanukah
if he would light the candles
on a little Menorah and speak Hebrew
to his country Christian friends.
As we sat around the campfire,
embers flickered in our eyes,
and Ben told the story of the Feast of Lights,
one generation from the night of broken glass.

Hometown Apocalyptic, 1965

Great blue herons drifted in the still air,
my father lost his job, and my mother wept
into dishwater as she stared out the kitchen
window into the mulberry tree forming its

tiny fruit. My sister dated a boy with tattoos,
and Father McCatherty got lost in confession,
and the rest of us seemed lost too, hovering
the cloaked door of our own confessionals,

priestless, relying on a merciful God, who
had spoken creation into being, to listen.
Crops scorched early, ponds dried up,
and storefront preachers pranced like ponies

as they spoke of apocalyptic happenings
and the nothing that happened in our
little town was as apocalyptic and normal
as scorched crops and the periodic curse of locust.

Despite warnings, no pyramids were built,
no doors were blood-marked, but the first born sons
were taken by the army for the latest war,
and the Red Sea parted to let negro children

from the bottoms attend white schools,
White Only signs were removed from courthouses
and bus stations as little Christian academies
sprang up on the outskirts of town.

Father Rousky replaced Father McCatherty
who got a job teaching the classics,
and Aunt Prudence went to Confessional.
My father got a new job, my mother wept

in dishwater as she stared out the window
at the loaded mulberry tree filled with waxwings,
and the drift of herons, dawn and dusk, continued
down the Obion River toward the Mississippi.

Shotgun

Have you ever heard a gun blast and witnessed
birdshot like a flock of tiny starlings
speeding through the air in ordered chaos,
seeking whatever blocks its path?
That morning a group of town boys escaped

to the bottoms where the Forked Deer River
flows into the Mississippi, their new Christmas shotguns
oiled and ready. After assassinating a ditch of beer cans,
an occasional unlucky crow and a case of Ball jars
stolen from some mother's cupboard, they turned their guns

on a shack edging two thousand acres of crop stubble,
not suspecting someone actually lived there.
First the windows shattered into jagged shards,
then the front door, again and again until the center
splintered and through the hole a stuffed mattress

appeared, and a kitchen counter with three coffee cans
filled with flour, sugar and lard. When new shots rang out,
sparkles scattered, hog-fat bled the walls like tallow
and a white cloud hung in the air, then blanketed
two pine chairs and a table. They spared a picture

of a snaggle-toothed girl in a flour sack dress,
but the mattress was vulnerable. Three shots later
goose feathers and newspaper confettied the room.
Two boys who had stood by watching this destruction
ran to an open jeep and scratched off down the dirt road.

One of the shooters aimed and fired. The driver saw
the cloud in his side mirror, followed by a scald so hot
he knew he'd been branded. The jeep rolled in a ditch
and the boy fell out of the driver's seat. It took the Doc
an hour to pick the pellets from his ears. Of course

the sharecropper returned and the sheriff was called.
The boys' fathers, glad to rebuild the shack,
made the boys sign a written apology and attend
Sunday School for a month. Have you ever wished
you could reach back forty years and tell the privileged

about the nothing some folks ever own? They were
your ears, old friend, but it's me that remembers
after a truck backfire on the morning road. I sip coffee
on the porch and make up little speeches I could
have used instead of standing with my hands in my pockets.

But that won't erase the plink of shot hitting
the doctor's metal tray, and the long drought
of weathering my father's judgment. Sometimes
I'd like to slip the safety off, pull back the hammer—
feel my finger on the trigger, take aim at the past.

Razing Hell

—for Ross

All shall be well, and
All manner of thing shall be well.
—T. S. Eliot, "Little Gidding"

I couldn't spell shitt without two t's.
Sixteen, wide-eyed and innocent, ready
to ride a bus from West Tennessee
to visit a friend at the University
of the South at Sewanee. I wrote
that I wanted to raze hell, and he
responded that Baptists were deeply
impressed with my theology.
It would be years before I understood
his joke. I was reading *Catcher in the Rye*
and thought I was Holden Caulfield.

We cooked pieces of steak over a candle
in his dorm room and ate slices of fresh
bread with butter. Later I drank 5 beers
in a fraternity house and threw up
in the yard, my loyal friend holding
my bucking shoulders. After high school,

I flunked out of college and lived
in a commune in California.
Ross graduated with honors, got drafted
and ended up a medic in Vietnam.
He wrote how the army botched
his hemorrhoid surgery, how it took
a blood-sweating hour to take a crap.

No wonder he went AWOL, sought shelter
in the Anglican Church. They smuggled
him to England where he lived in a monastery.
How fitting, his favorite poem, "Little Gidding"
From "The Four Quartets." He read it to me
when I was seventeen and explained Eliot's
vision of the Holy Spirit. Years later, Ross
repatriated; the army gave him a discharge,
not honorable, not dishonorable.

He returned a man of the cloth, an Episcopal
priest dying of leukemia. I was the only pallbearer
at his funeral who knew him. His best friend,
Bubba Hawls, sat in his motorcycle jacket and jeans
under the scrutiny of small town myopia.

I remember the summer Ross and I drove
the back roads drinking wine and pissing
in the dark gravel beside the car. He,
who could crack a limerick on any subject,
sang to me his holy Latin hymns
in an Irish countertenor. How we fall
into friendships that never quite define
themselves doesn't matter. Death,

fill his Heaven with Yeats and Bach.
Make a back road lined with cottonwoods
that leads to the Mississippi. Conjure
a stone cathedral with a slate roof where
dead poets and saints rise up to recite
verse and bless lambs and people of honor.
Ross, my little father, you are still my priest.
I may never spell shitt without two t's,
but if I could, I'd raze hell for you.

Back When

I say *back when*
                    and the words
go to North West Tennessee –
slow moving water,
                    brown, browner
as little rivers stream a muddy sky
                    toward the Mississippi.

Cypress and tupelo sloughs,
                    ducks in winter,
snakes in summer,
                    and always mosquitoes
and always song birds.

                    Gutted trailers
stacked with hay,
                    white beans and cornbread
and chicken on Sundays.

                    Little country clubs,
golf courses, pickups,
                    and poverty—
black poverty and white poverty,
                    and, Sweet Jesus,
church music, honky-tonk,
                    and church music
and sweat, always sweat,
                    and hard work
if you can get it,
                    and beer joints
where you can nurse
                    a beer all night,

and still say
> the words nigger

and wetback,
> and go home stupid,

and wake up sad,
> and never wake up.

THE FOUR-SECOND RULE

We followed it in our house—
if food dropped on the floor,
you could eat it if harvested
within four seconds. As kids,
my sister and I stood close
to our mother when she sliced
ham or grated cheese. More
than a game, it was a reward
for diligence in a hungry world.
The four-second rule spread
to privileges outside—you
could ride shotgun if you
called it in time, or shoot first
in a pickup game, or choose
to receive in football without
a coin toss. We thought that
God made the universe in as
little time. But the four-second rule
stopped at the neighborhood edge.
We had to stand in line at school,
rope around the dusty floors
and listen to old Miss Hornbuckle
dress us down. *Young Man,*
she yelled at me, and I learned
early that words didn't mean
what the dictionary said, and that
everyone's kitchen floor wasn't
as clean as my mother's. In the
army the cook spit on the biggest
dessert so no one would eat it.
I read today that there are 1600
diet books in circulation,
that our country spends a million
dollars a minute on war, and

every two seconds a person starves
to death somewhere on the planet.
Oh, to be young and innocent
watching mother fix supper
and snatch a piece of cheese
without two hearts stopping.

Lake County, West Tennessee

At first they are snow geese
    flown from Isom Lake,
but no, white plastic bags,
    scores of them captured
by the sharp fingers of harvested
    cotton stubble.
A thousand acres of furrows
    taper into the distance,
one shotgun shack vagrants the corner,
    its windows jagged,
porch fallen in, a well pump
    and two hogs rooting hardscrabble.
Something desolate abides
    in a cotton field tattooed
with plastic bags—
    surrender flags escaped
from the strip mall grocery
    at the edge of a dying town,
each waving
    Save A Lot
Save A Lot   Save A Lot

The Varsity Sweater

My father's sweater sits on the closet shelf.
It scored a few moth holes over the years,
folded neatly, rough collar open to the dark.

I take it down to show grandkids, to spark
ritual memories with my brothers and sister.
It is red with a gray U in the center

for Union University. He was a tailback,
hard, slight and fast. The yearbook
nicknamed him Farmer Brown. At seventeen

I found the sweater in a cedar trunk
while combing through drawers for college.
As small as I was, I barely pulled it

over my torso. The sleeves wound
my wrist like handcuffs, the collar a noose.
I could hang myself in my father's sweater

or straitjacket jumbled dreams that surf
my childhood: his pre-dawn sigh to start
the furnace, the shadows of jays screaming

in the yard, the sandpaper chin that awkwardly
kissed us, Hank Williams songs in the shower,
weary mechanic's hands tucking me in good night,

the smell of L&Ms on the porch after supper,
smoke rings rising into darkness, footprints
of crows in the fallen snow of his death.

Landscapes, a Meditation

When my father was a boy, the bluff above the river
was so deep with hardwoods that night lanterns
couldn't fill the darkness. Each cabin was a mere
flicker in the trees. Tonight on our country ridge
every house has its street lamp to chase away
what hides in shadows. The stars have been pushed
further into a sky, which all the hydroelectric
and power plants can't keep from falling.

Hopper painted isolation haloing human scenes.
He knew the light of the diner couldn't save
the night hawks from chaos at the edge of the frame.
Wyeth understood weathered barns and houses,
so human in their textured brush strokes, spoke truth
of life in Maine, unlike his skies, swept beyond
interpretation. He knew how lonely we become
inside appointed roles: distraction, a hobby,
solitude, a house of mirrors.

I long to return to boyish dawns on Reelfoot Lake—
open sky reflected on the surface, where a snag
in the distant mist turned into a heron through
some alchemy of light and water, a time when
definition mattered less than discovery. Evenings,
the sun fired the western edge before it dropped into
the Mississippi. I would find the North Star on what
my father called the drinking gourd, offer up my heart
with a chorus of whippoorwills, and let distant
cypress trees above Deep Slough be my horizon.

Tonight, Alone

Tonight is a room with a window
    that holds my mother's face.
She would have pulled the curtains
    to keep strangers blind to our habits.
I keep it open, sit on the bed and watch her eyes
    glisten with moon glare,
her rose garden unpruned, her love
    and disapproval rising like a flash flood—
how perfect we could never be,
    but for her, we tried.

Tonight is a 49 Chevy
    with a fractured mirror
that holds my father's face.
    From the back seat
where my sister and I watched cotton fields
    stubble the delta landscape
and naked poles count the miles,
    his broken eyes hold a gentleness.
Honesty was his silence, his prayers answered
    for everyone but himself.

To be alive is to welcome memories,
    good and bad. Like the morning cries of crows,
they call us to the gift of living.
    But tonight, faces and places
hang in my closet like well-worn clothes.
    I pour a glass of wine and try each on—
always amazed at the comfort of old sorrows
    and their clumsy familiar fit.

III

THE DANCE

The Dance

I would have the day
pass through me as
Cane Creek passes

through the landscape
to meet the river—
to be a bed of

stones and sand,
reeds and mosses
quilting my body.

To be still, stationary,
as the earth dogs
its circle around the sun.

I don't pause,
but am pause
in this flux,

more ponderous
than sycamores
arching their milk arms

over the stream
which I cradle,
my shoulders

like limestone,
the slow immeasurable
wearing away,

informing my matter
which cannot settle,
nor keep from spinning.

Long Division

Walking beside Sulfur Fork Creek
a great blue heron stalks the shallows,
the shapes of painted turtles rise,
and a queen snake suns on a rock.

I think of poor Adam and his job of naming.
Even in the Tennessee hills the task is endless.
What was Yahweh thinking?
Some of the names must have come easy—

swallowtail, luna moth, bluebird,
violet, hearts-a-busting. But every bacteria,
slime mold, lichen? Even the slider
slipping into the water keeps its promise

to thrive and multiply. In this magical world
of physics and chemistry—do the math—
divide backwards by any number
and never reach the zero in creation.

I would look up the exact scripture
but my wife is using my Bible
to press wild flowers—columbine,
anemone, flame azalea, larkspur.

Wednesday Miracles

Driving down the ridge, I watch a meadow
of chicory shimmer in the breeze like a lake.

From a closer view, thistle and goldfinches
speckle the floral waves pink, black and yellow.

Some mornings miracles dress themselves
like Renoir's *Little Girl in Blue*. Today

I choose to believe in miracles—a flash
of indigo bunting in the sun, a child making faces

in a car window, while her mother argues on a cell,
throws me a kiss. I catch it and send it back.

On this Wednesday I'm forgiving everyone—
the mother on the phone, the truck that cut me off,

even the raucous crow that mocks forgiveness.
Like me, it knows we need more forgiveness

than we can gift. Shouldn't it be that way?
Humbled by desire to come clean, to finally

have it out with belief, we admit that belief
is perhaps worth the doubt it takes to get there,

and doubt involves a dangerous caring. But not
on a day of miracles when a field of chicory

becomes a mountain lake dressed in the hues
of Renoir's painting—a blue clad girl

with golden hair absorbed in a book.
Who can't believe on a morning

when indigo buntings masquerade as sun gods
and a child throws a stranger her kiss.

Raccoon

At night while my wife and I read,
a large banging on the porch has us
at the window. A mother raccoon
and young are busy looting as our
cats watch with interest from a rail.
She orders her kits to dismantle
the hummingbird feeders, stuff fists
full of sunflower seed in snouts,
then escape dragging the suet cage
into the woods never to return, my
porch walls a nicely honeyed mess.
"Raccoon" comes from the Algonquian—
aroughcoune, arathkone. The Sioux
called them *spotted face,* sharp and cunning,
who in legend played dead beside a river
until a tribe of crayfish, in festive dress,
came to feast, but were feasted on
instead. My wife laughs at their antics.
She loves them. I'm not so sure.

Raccoon, your Ojibway name
is *grasper, they pick up things,*
Iroquois, *masked demon spirit,*
Dakota, *magic one with painted face.*
Today as you slumber with your young,
will you dream for me: perhaps a creek full
of crayfish, or a carnival house of mirrors
reflecting distorted faces that have me
wrestle sheets until I wake with a gasp,
revenge for my boyhood cap with a
ringed tail streaming down the back
or roadsides rag-matted with fur
and scatter bones. The Aztecs called

you *she who talks with spirits.* Talk
for us, *grasper, magic one, spotted face,*
Kabuki Omnivore. Tell them we are selfish,
careless, even reckless. Tell them I am sorry.

To the Dead Opossum on the Roadside

How many mornings, stuffed with carrion
and grubs, rattail stiff as a coil, you smiled
your way into a hollow log to drift through
the bright day in shadowed slumber.

Most ancient of mammals, queen of natural
selection, pouched marsupial, you lie covered
with mown grass, a scraggle of fur, less
than a ragamuffin, the bloating ceased,

the maggots' fury vacated, no more hymnal
of green flies, just a whit of hide and a few
teeth attached to an odd snout. Broken
little engine that can't, slugabed Buddha,

spared the tripe of tired theology, rest now,
content once to be and now not to be.

The Little Blue Corporal

It's rare to see a merlin on the ridge,
bigger than a kestrel, but not quite
a peregrine. Watch it hunt and you'll
learn how it earned that name. First,
identify the prey, then fly off slow,
not to affright it. Then dart it,
that quick, that clean, sometimes
screaming ki-ki-ki, or byk-byk-byk.
Legend has Merlin born of woman,
sired by an incubus, that mysterious
immortal that seduces females
in their sleep. Some tales have
Merlin a wise wizard, others
a madman. In my short life
of spiritual groping, I used
to imagine a world in which
every creature that strove to be
its best would win another life
in a higher form. I understand
this desire in a cockroach, aardvark
or human, but why would a merlin
want to be anything else? Falconers
call the male "The Little Blue Corporal"
in its brown and slate blue uniform;
our desire, perhaps, to dress a creature
we admire in human garb. There he goes—
off the snag, winging low to the ground,
then a burst of speed, up and gone,
that clean, that quick.

Coyotes, Lake County, Colorado

Hearing coyotes in the high Rockies
reminds me of a celebration or a wake.
A friend working for a Texas senator
once showed me a picture of a rancher
with twenty dead coyotes strung on barbed wire,
the constituent's case for automatic rifles.
My friend shook his head, "Texas," he said.
All I thought about was those silent howls:
shrill cries, squeaks, and elongated blues.
You can hear little ones tuning up,
their muzzles raised to the orange of evening
when sage becomes numerous shades of green,
cottonwoods re-enact creation over rivers,
and aspen leaves lift off the earth like a burst
of birds breaking a ridge.

My wife, who has never heard such howls,
sits with amazement at the window.
Call me romantic, tree-hugging, whatever.
I don't have sheep with lambs in high pasture,
but I have heard their innocent bleats,
have been charmed by their comic rampages.
I have eaten their chops rare in fine cafes.
It's about commerce: personal, collective, human,
and justified. I can't imagine a night among the mine
slag and distorted hills without coyotes. My neighbor
has lost pigs to them. He has no use for coyotes,
and that's the point. You can't raise them,
you can't sell them, and sometimes they interfere
with the animals you do.

All I know is that for the last five nights
as the sunset painted a red haze around
the Mount Massive Wilderness, God's dogs

have raised a chorus so perfect for this landscape,
so beyond the affairs of humans, to close the day
like you close the last page of a good book,
finished but over too soon.

Solomon's Ants

Go to the ant, thou sluggard; consider her ways, and be wise
—Proverbs 6:6

Part of the order of Hymenoptera,
cousin to wasps and bees—

Hymen, the goddess of marriage,
perhaps you were named

for your desirable shapes—
thin waist, rounded bulbous parts.

You are ruled by queens, birthed
by queens, sired by drones, and

supported by sterile female workers.
Some of you grow large and deadly,

others as lowly as piss ants.
What god would have us follow

your example? You've had
130 million years to perfect

your communes. Some colonies
a million strong, you jog through

earthly routines as if work was heaven.
How lovely to be of one mind.

Come to us wise ones:
teach us to live without desire;

teach us to live without sorrow;
teach us to make our artfulness

as functional as sweat shops,
assembly lines; teach us

to be numb to the plight of those
who do not ensure our success.

Symbolism

> *The Cross, the Crown, the Scales may all*
> *As well have been the Sword.*
> —Robert Frost

Four scruffy vultures on a sycamore snag
above Walker Creek could be symbols
of death—their zoom-in eyes stare
at a decaying doe in the roadside ditch.

"Something dies, something lives,"
my father said. But natural selection
isn't much on symbolism. Vultures
don't care if the car that hit the deer

is part of nature. Supply and demand,
like the homeless raiding the garbage cans
outside of McDonalds. It gives trickle
down economics new meaning when

children are hungry. The street vet pulls
his Vietnam cap over his toboggan.
His dead visit too often for him to have
time to work. A certain sound and he's

reliving a village strewn with bodies
after the chemical fire rained,
or a buddy with a hole
where an eye should be.

Symbolism is human—flag,
crescent moon, cross, star of David—
the need for something
to stand for something else.

The Short List (in no certain order)

> *Poets, like whores, are only hated by each other.*
> —William Wycherly

How could I hate
Wilbur for his laundry,
Thomas for his hill,
Kinnell for his bear,
Lowell for his skunk,
Oliver for her humpbacks?

And what about
Rich's wreck,
Frost's directive,
Dickinson's formal,
Auden's beaux arts
Whitman's ferry,
Keats's autumn,
Coleridge's domes,
Blake's innocence,
Blake's experience?

Without Shelley's wind,
could I fly?
Without Byron's ruins,
could I love?
Without Yeats's lake,
could I be homesick?
Without Stevens's paramour,
could be be enough?

Bishop's art, Sexton's storm, Plath's jar,
have taught me how to lose, how to fear,
how not to die.
No poet works like Levine,
and oh, to borrow Kunitz's dust.

The Light

Beware of prosperity, friend, and seek affection.
    —Charles Wright

Driving to the library to write a poem,
the poem writes itself. Get the yellow
legal pad she says, and the blue ink pen.
I prefer blue—the sky is blue, October blue—
the ocean is blue, though you haven't
taken me in a year. The water in the mall
fountain is fake blue which is only fitting.
I turn onto the beltway around the city,
the yellow pad on the steering wheel.
In the library café, I get a cup of coffee
and sit by the window. The poem
stares into the park on Church Street
where the homeless warm in the sun.
One man lights two cigarettes in his mouth
and hands one to a friend who thanks
him with a palm on his shoulder.
Even the homeless love each other,
the poem says. A boy with a terrible
scar on his face pulls a piece of paper
from his pocket, unfolds the creases
with care and begins to read. He knows
the words by heart, the poem says,
but reads the letter moving his lips
so he can see the hand that wrote them,
so a constellation is lit of her fingers,
her eyes, her mouth. The poem watches
a cabbage butterfly dance the air
above a rose bush. A legless old woman
in a motorized chair stops at the cross-walk
on Church and 5th. The poem reaches
over and takes my hand, each of us
is waiting for a light to change, she says.

Pragmatic Angel

While reading at the kitchen table,
my wife says, "I need to measure
a space for an angel" (I pause to listen)
"to place between your parents' graves."
But hearing *angel*, I hoped for
something different—Gabriel's
bright light reflected in the kitchen
window, or hung in the closet where
we could kneel to plead his blessing,
or perched on the roof to greet
me home from work—
angels armed with hair dryers
to melt so many frozen hearts,
or icemakers to save the polar bears.
Oh angels, give tax breaks to people
of kindness, or holy magic words
to turn war planes into manna delivery.
I want to know how one measures
a space for an angel, how small
a tape to calculate a pin's head?
But standing in the family plot
of our hometown cemetery—
"with quick cement," my wife says,
"eight and a half by eleven."

The Stolen Day

Out of the dusk strewn sky,
out of the dark shadows
cottonwoods cast on the river bank,

shaped by the sounds of beetles
banging the porch screen, tree frogs,
and the trailing hymns of trucks

headed south on the highway,
evening took the day from me.
The same day that had found me

staring at the rustling window shades
as the eastern sky lit the dew-
stained forest beside the house.

Evening stole the day from me,
filed its scenes, artifacts, and scraps
of talk as dream fossils, and still,

out of all this, your face will not die
as you have died, is not diminished
as the fist of ashes spread down

the old barn road, by the spring house,
under the willow where you watched
watercress build its summer home.

Lullaby

Shade becomes shadows,
maple leaves, small hands,
not waving or reaching,
but each dangling like a child's
who sleeps without dreaming.
Sleep now, sleep.

It being May, mulberries
grow green and new,
tight against their shady stems.
No one could imagine
them ripe and purple.
Sleep now, sleep.

Shepherd and lamb words spoken—
fists full of dirt dropped
in such a tiny grave
seem to cause tremors
like an aftershock.
Sleep now, sleep.

Cars at the cemetery
encircle like a wagon train
in a cowboy movie, to protect
something fragile.
The battle is over.
Sleep now, sleep.

The Living

> *It's the living who cannot*
> *live without the dead…*
> —Hilda Morley

The older we become the more we look like them,
and it's not just physical: Mother's brown eyes,

Father's big ears, Grandfather's red hair,
but in how the eyes stare past the kitchen table

to the open window, how the chin seems made
for the palm, or how we learn to point without pointing

the way our mother did when she heard whispers
in another room. Remember our mother's funeral,

we kept speaking in present tense as if she were
out to check the mail. The living practice

not being embarrassed when a stranger asks
the wrong question. "Oh, she's dead," isn't

the right answer—the person starts apologizing
while you apologize for her apology.

After my father's fatal heart attack,
a man knocked on the door, asked for him,

so he could unload a car in his service garage.
Seeing me speechless, my sister quipped,

"Oh, he doesn't work there anymore."
Then under her breath, "He's busy tuning

St. Peter's Chevy." In time we share the ritual
of telling our dead's stories: their horse, their dog,

the marriage, the fire, the storm, the war.
The dead are major players in them all,

except, of course, their last one,
which we learn to shoulder on our own.

Watering the Herbs

Start with the Greek oregano, a symbol of honor,
used to decorate newlyweds, to banish sadness,
to repel serpents—if only Eve had known.
Then to the lemon grass, a soother of ligaments,
a spice for Asian foods. I rub leaves between
my fingers, and the yellow fruit rise up in me—
lemonade stands of childhood, St. John Ave., a nickel
a glass. I turn to the mint, my wife's favorite.
Oh Menthe, most beautiful nymph,
when you thought to seduce Pluto,
Proserpine turned you into an herb.
How the god's vindictiveness has enriched our flora.
I lift the hose to keep from over watering
and spy the pungent Karti. In Hebrew, eaten
at Rosh Hashanah, *to cut off enemies:*
Shalom, peace be unto thee little leeks.
Finally, my pesto beauties, green, green basil;
your name from the basilink, half lizard,
half dragon, a creature with a fatal piercing stare.
You protect us from the evil eye. My grandmother
called it *the look,* when she whispered stories
about the hag that lived in Dismal Hollow.
How precious the storied language of plants; a walk
in the woods, and names rise from the forest loam:
bloodroot, hepatica, hyssop, heal all, hoary puccoon—
millennia of legends, cures, curses in a thousand tongues:
a god turns himself into a lecherous swan, a princess
is stolen into winter, an arrogant hero falls in love
with his reflection and drowns. Children on every
continent are lured into darkness by the evil-eyed hag,
lost forever among the infamous glory of words.

Frame

Even as we watched from my writing class
a man kick the trashcan in front of school,
yelling *I will not eat your fucking garbage,*
my students had the decency not to laugh,

but to settle into their desks to write.
One student, a Hindu girl, asked to be
excused, and we watched her at the curb
give the man her sack lunch. I remember

thinking at the time, that we can begin
and end each day with *even:* even
as the sun crests the eastern edge of
the ridge, a peregrine swoops from

the gargoyle on the Commerce building
and takes a pigeon from the street; even
as the sun melts the horizon like an egg
yolk, the old woman pushes her rubble

from 8th Avenue into the alley full
of dumpsters, and one has to admire
how sweetly she cares for the faded baby-
doll in the child seat of her grocery cart.

The Ten Most Violent Cities

Out my window
the last hickory leaves
and the rounded hulls
of squirrels' nests
decorate winter trees.
A late November
wind rattles limbs
and tatters dance,
tiny marionettes,
their songs muted
secrets I can't glean.
The headlines list
the ten most violent cities.
I doubt if they know
the ten most peaceful.
I leave the paper
on the kitchen table
and go outside
to rake leaves.
It's a flannel morning,
soft cotton checkered
against the skin.
A sudden break
in clouds spotlights
the sun that too
soon fades to gray.
The heart, an old man
dressed in brogans
and faded trousers,
searches the sky for rain,
translates the barred owl
that haunts the forest edge:
no need for news today.

Today

Up the ridge my neighbor's goats
stare from the cab of an old pickup.
Their heads poke out the missing windshield
long since trampled into chert.
The hood's vestiges of blue paint
pale beside a scatter of cornflowers.

The goats and I watch helicopters breach the ridge,
then disappear, trailing choppy thunder south.
Most likely, soldiers think Iraq and Afghanistan,
not goats, flowers, and goldfinches
come to harvest thistle and timothy.

In the dust and rubble of Baghdad,
women, wrapped in their rook-black
sorrow, wave their hands and grieve;
tears stream through thick beards of men
loading dead and wounded into trucks.
"The horror, the horror," Marlon Brando whispered
in *Apocalypse Now*. I remember the film shifting
to a man butchering a steer. I remember
my brother's silence when he returned from Vietnam.

The goats jump from the truck and jerk at tall grass
beneath the fence. Like me, they seem pleased,
left to the meadowlark's call and the rude antics
of crows. I think of Wendell Berry—his poem
about the night he heard more war news
and left his house to sow fescue in the pasture.

So today I'll plant the seedling sycamore
my niece gave to us for Arbor Day.
I'll visit the goats and watch their kid—
she toddles when she runs—for that chance
she'll let me hold her in my arms.

IV

The Calling

This Poem

We never signed up for this lottery—
tornados, lightning strikes, spider bites—
droughts and floods. We could easily blame
the earth for our sorrows. After being awake all night
listening to Storm Tracker watch twenty twisters
blister Tennessee, I take coffee to the porch
and find my trellis bright with morning glories.

For the infant buried in trailer rubble,
for the mill worker whose home was flattened,
for the CEO airlifted from the roof
of her drowned Mercedes,
    I write this poem.

For my worthless cats who hunt butterflies,
for my mother who waits for dead relatives to visit,
for the raccoons who wreck my bird feeders,
for my tomato plants red with fruit,
    I write this poem.

For the little brown bat that embraces darkness,
for the whippoorwills who lay their eggs
in the peril of the forest loam,
for the raucous crows who document death,
    I write this poem.

For the eye sockets of deer skulls,
for empty turtle shells,
for the hulls of cicadas,
for all of the bones and exoskeletons
that decorate this hallowed grave—
miraculous, terrible, lovely and unjust,
    I wake in the deepest part of night
      and write this poem.

I, whose bones will one day fold into ashes,
    fall to my knees
      and write this poem.

What the Wind Says

Nothing much in early June
before heat excites thermals
that shake the forest crown.
Wind won't apologize—
disturbing is its business.
It speaks by curling
the edges of the porch,
shearing the window
with its palms, fingering
pine needles, caressing
the surface of water
until drops leap up
into spray.

The wind loves smoke
and dust and vapor—
anything that shapes
and tosses, so free
to follow its course.
Like children's dreams,
before they're taught
what isn't possible,
the wind is essential
and dangerous. What
brings the healing rains
and soars the eagles
erodes stone, fuels fires
and flattens houses.

Who, who am I
wind asks the hollow rock—
the sleet that belts
the roof answers
and the limb that scratches

the midnight window,
and the morning breeze
that shutters light through maples
and the dreams of chlidren
who too soon forget its song.

The Calling

Something calls above the tops of trees:
not exactly the wind, or crows having

their morning disagreement; not my dead
whose voices I remember like the smell

of biscuits, the taste of molasses and butter;
not would-be lovers and their lonely fingers,

but a clear calling, one of October blue
and crisp air; one of heavy dew dripping

from gum and maple like rain; not lowland fog
that whispers to grass; not my childhood friends

who, living or dead, still dwell in the land
of leaf piles and trees, complaining

to the sky when their mothers call them home.
Not a song, but a calling like the circle

a hawk makes, or the dull moon in daylight,
or the fire and purple rings after looking

at the sun. I strain to hear the voice
of bright unopened moments, but how can

I listen to what was almost said: the sound
of a girl's hair that never touched my pillow,

the poem I forgot in some airport in Kansas,
the words I imprisoned until my father died.

Two Unanswered Questions

> *And if the earthly no longer knows your name...*
> —Rilke

> *Nothing that is not there and the nothing that is...*
> —Wallace Stevens

What were they thinking,
    the old ones
        being wheeled about
            the nursing home garden;

the black-eyed Susans
    reminding them of the flood
        of '37 when the last red wolves
            were driven from the bottoms,

or how Sister
    would pull the petals,
        he loves me,
            he loves me not?

What were they thinking,
    the sycamore leaves
        in the summer storm,
            the ones blown

to the creek
    leaving their
        veined prints
            upon the stones?

Tapping

Today out walking, I stop to listen
to the tapping of cottonwood leaves
beside Sulfur Fork Creek and remember
my wife's story about her mother.

She sat on the porch swing tapping
and tapping her heels on the wooden floor.
What are you doing, Mother, my wife asked?
I'm tapping out my sadness, she said.

And I wanted to know how many taps
for being abandoned with small children
during a Michigan winter, or her second
husband's slow death from cancer;

how many taps for her grandson's
violence and addiction. But no, today
her tapping, she says, is for her niece
and new baby who cancelled a visit.

And I think, perhaps it's the daily
disappointments, the lost chances
that save her present from final dementia—
the blessed names she can't unearth

from the wreckage of memory,
the nameless sorrows that decorate
all of our dreams. I sit in cottonwood shade
to listen to the tapping of leaves

as they swivel in the breeze,
a design of natural selection to
preserve moisture in time of drought.
I celebrate the cottonwoods' survival,

and my wife's mother, who,
though losing her words daily,
sits on the porch swing tapping,
tapping away her sadness.

Gravid

There is something earthen in late August.
Rains come and go, but nothing sustains the soil,
the chest. A weighing cramps the shoulders,

stoops a person. The very idea of gravity
must have occurred before Newton.
The persimmon trees are gravid, my heart

is gravid, but births nothing in late August—
no C-section for that little metaphor,
and like most, no true comparisons, except

in the weight of words, enslaved as they are,
to wrestle with feelings. The hawk cries along
the biome between woods and pasture—

hungry, it cries, hungry for change. The hollow
chest swells when thermals surprise the maple,
and clouds block the sun. My cats don't care

for dog days. They lie in the shade, cranky
as creek mud. The word dog is pronounced
in two syllables in August.

Even the mockingbird and crow stretch vowels,
and chalk from gravel roads would have Dante
add another concentric circle to hell.

The praying mantis performs leg positions
that would cripple a contortionist. And,
heartsick, I'm straining to pray as well.

Heart

Keep thy heart with all diligence: for out of it are the issues of life.
—Proverbs 4:23

Oh, Solomon, such a large job
for such a small engine, fist-sized,
a lump of clay—born beating
from the womb to last 80 years.

So maybe it deserves to be
the grand metaphor that makes
editors gag, and cynics laugh.
Well, let them laugh, little muscle—

like the high school students
who laughed at *Schindler's List*.
Is it the bomb tonnage, the flies
figure skating starving eyes,

generations of unkept promises?
So much is broken. Yet, today
on the greenbelt, children squeal
as they feed geese, lovers hold hands

and shyly avoid each others' eyes,
and a young father bucks his daughter
on his shoulders like a bronco.
It's hard writing a creek poem

without a heron and the drift of clouds.
It's hard to watch a fireman on CNN
burn his hands and face saving a child
from a flaming van. *My job*, he says.

In the Orthopedic Clinic

CNN announces nine firefighters
    lost when a burning
    roof collapsed.

A pregnant woman is missing
    in Ohio—feared kidnapped
    in front of her small son.

A flashflood in Texas
    swept an infant
    from its mother's arms.

A truck bomb in Iraq
    kills dozens at a mosque
    north of Baghdad.

The nurse calls my name—
    it's time for my annual
    hip x-ray.

I know the routine—
    lie down, put your toes together,
    stay still, don't breathe, breathe—

turn your knee out,
    hold still,
    don't breathe, breathe.

I wait for the doctor in room four,
    wonder how many disasters
    I've missed—

another girl raped in Darfur,
    a starving child in the Congo,
    a man trapped

in an elevator in Toledo,
    undocumented workers
    found dead in the desert.

Doctor Shell comes in,
    says my hip is worn out—
    needs replacement—

When the pain
    keeps me awake at night,
    he can fix it.

Hip Surgery

When the doctor said hip surgery,
I thought, this is cool—a little jazz,
a black turtleneck, a glass of cabernet.
It could take place in an old hippie bus
painted paisley with sunflowers and peace signs.
Then I saw the x-rays—hip, the largest joint
in the body. Look—no cartilage, bone on bone,
no wonder it hurts like hell—
this joint my ass is attached to.

Three days in the hospital, the sexy therapist,
Nadia, has me walk 100 steps the first day.
Lay down she says, put your legs together—
now pinch your butt for 5 seconds—
do this 20 times. At home—two weeks on a walker,
then a cane, then I walk two miles at the park.

A card arrives for use at airports—
an alarm goes off when the metal cap
walks through security. I feel the alien
when I sit. I'll be hiking soon.
It will be hip—Duke hip, Monk hip,
Van Morrison hip, this space age hip.
At 59 I can pinch my butt 60 times
in 3 minutes, just for you, Nadia.

My Niece and I Listen to Jazz

It's *round midnight*
and Cannonball Adderley's
deep sax mines dark matter
of the heart, and my niece
starts singing the words.
"I lose the music when
you sing," I say. But she
wants to *know what love is*,
she wants to be a *funny valentine*,
she wants to sit on Chet's lap
and put her ear to his chest.
I want to hear his trumpet.
I want the slant keys of Bill Evans
plinking the bones in my spine,
I want to feel Coltrane count
neutron stars before they implode.
She asks why they write lyrics
if you're not supposed to sing.
She really doesn't need my reply.
She wants to sing *let's get lost*,
she wants *her love here to stay*.
I need to hear maestro Monk
share his stage. "I'm *kinda blue*,"
I tell her, "I've got Miles to blow
before I sleep." But we settle on
Ella scat, Mel scat and listen
to Sarah Vaughn whose shrill vocals
tempt musicians to case their horns.

Subtext

When you died, it was easier to keep breathing
than to stop and try to start again, even as
I boarded a plane away from your death.
The sun rose above the Boise front frosting
sage with silver, painting scorched grass orange.
Two thousand miles east, it was 7 a.m. and I imagined
my brothers and sister telling your stories
as they readied for the funeral. How silly
I felt asking teachers in the Institute to write
about their pivotal moments. How silly I felt
explaining the importance of tension in poetry,
how every story must start in the middle,
how the silence beneath words must deafen the reader.
My pulse drowned the clock which counted down the day.
The late Idaho light led me beside the cool river where
cottonwoods coated the greenbelt with summer snow,
reminding me of my Tennessee childhood. The desert night,
when it came, held a face heavy with stars.

Planting Iris

Grief should squat in the petunias
    like a toad
while you separate root stock
    left in a paper sack
by your mother. June,
    the wrong time, she would warn,
to plant iris,
    but it won't get done
hidden in a dark corner
    of the basement.
She'll still be dead.
    So the toad waits patiently
in the petunias, proud
    of its blemishes and bumps.
If you cradle it in your hands
    it will pee, causing warts
your mother warned—just like
    the ones you had when
you were a boy.
    So you stare into
the little Buddha's eyes
    until they blink.
By August the iris will
    sprout green kitten ears.
They won't bloom this year.

Weeding

Weeding poke and love vine
       from my garden,
I'm careful not to jerk
       impatiens and daisies.
I lift the leaves of columbine
       and the delicate shoots
of bleeding hearts to stunt the grass
       sprouted since the last rain.
When my father was at war
       in the Pacific,
mother would weed her roses
       and call out the names
of islands where men had fallen—
       Hawaii, Iwo Jima, Guam,
and tear the intruders by the roots,
       ejecting them
against her helplessness
       to bring my father home.

So this morning before coffee
       and the headline news,
I use the cool of the day
       to tear weeds with bare fingers—
Baghdad, Kirkuk,
       Afghanistan, Darfur, Gaza—
jerk up one weed
       at a time for thousands
who never heard the bombs falling,
       rip stems and shoots
against car bombs, assassins
       and religious fanatics,
at home and abroad,
       knowing from the start,
my hands are too frail,
       my garden too slight.

Talking to the Dust

To sit and be invisible—
        tell secrets to dust,
        how the kitten leaps

at its particles when sunlight
        breaches the window,
        how the preacher said *dust*

as often as *love* or *sin*,
        in the little church
        of my childhood.

Every Sunday I tried
        to be invisible, perched on
        the hard pew beside my mother

as I watched my father
        fall asleep in the choir.
        Dust to dust came near

the end of every sermon,
        no matter the theme.
        I wanted to be like God

and know the dust
        first hand, have it
        pass through me

the way ghosts pass through
        walls in old movies,
        or neutrinos through a planet.

While planting seeds, sifting dirt
        through my fingers,
        I speak to dust

as it clumps under my nails.
    I remember the little palms
    of dust we sprinkled

over my father's grave
    after the preacher said
    that *he fought the good fight.*

At sixteen,
    that meant little to me.
    Grief-sick, I turned to the heart songs

of Dylan, The Beatles and Joni Mitchell,
    unaware that at his death,
    he must have known

what he had to leave behind,
    uncertain of what he might join.
    Too soon my father became invisible.

This morning in my garden,
    I turn under the spent plants,
    drought stricken,

and ready the soil for fall greens.
    Older than my father,
    I know now how fortunate

I would be if someone said
    of me,
    he fought the good fight,

and through his conversations with dust,
    learned, not too late,
    a soft word, a gentle touch.

Pushing the Sky

Some people grow up pushing the sky,
with their fists, the heel of their hand
or with the sound and bluster of voices,
but what I like to do, my father said,
is walk out early morning on a day
butt-cold to the ankles, and let my breath
stream out and up as if the sky invited it,
welcomed it, as if the weight of the sky
wasn't pushing back. You learn— plowing
a fifty acre bottom in early spring—
to leave the sky to its own invention,
to let it wobble naked above you,
centered by a drift of clouds.
You learn even more on a battleship
in the Pacific, WWII, that a clear sky
is a terrible friend who changes opinions
like a squall on Reelfoot Lake—all blue
one moment and darkness rushing
your johnboat the next. But the sky
on the Tennessee River on a May morning
is more valuable than freshwater pearls
the mussel fishermen trade for whiskey.
You can pray to a sky like that, but it
won't do much good—there's a sky
above the sky above the sky, dazzling
in splendor of light and darkness.
Best to love the sky you have, if you
love your life, until it weighs you down,
as it will, in hopes that you have the grace
to stream your breath against the window,
watch how it fogs then disappears.

Descent

A sentinel of crows lines Cemetery Road,
a descent of souls spreads downhill

where the oldest stones are worn wordless.
Morning is worn as well with August dust,

corroded with locust trill. The rooster
barely chokes out a day. I seldom drive

this stretch anymore, no one to put a pot
of coffee on, just a parade of memories

stepping down the years. A grandmother,
red-faced, standing at a stove.

A hard-nosed judge of adults,
she never spoke unkindness to a child.

An old man on a horse followed
by a string of cows, a host of ghosts

who lived as surely as an after-supper tale.
Nights of river fishing for a run of stripes,

the shoreline crunch of mussel shells,
my father's lonesome tenor found and lost.

Some days an extra hour takes a detour,
turns left on memory's unmarked way

where loss has left a farmhouse jagged eyes,
the dogtrot stacked with wasted hay.

Ascent

In late September althea brightens yards of farmhouses,
morning glories adorn fences, and the deep purple
of ironweed lines the stubble of harvested corn.
Up Union Hill, long ago two churches joined
to heal a community wrecked by civil war.
Defended causes seemed lost in the mire of blood and bone.
Stones on the graveyard crown are nameless for a reason—
anonymous souls left for kind strangers to bury,
fieldstones wiped clean by time's mercy.
I stop and stroll through unmarked graves
to brush the dust from my father's brass plaque.
He was a veteran of the war in the Pacific.
Memory keepsakes its own markers—
a faded picture on a mantel,
a box seldom opened on a closet shelf,
an old shirt kept for planting a garden.
Despite a cloudless sky, perhaps souls are hesitant
to leave behind the smell of coffee, a child's handprint
on a window, how a lover's hair completes a pillow,
an April morning after a night of rain.

Crocker Springs

—in memory of Floyd Snow

I came to love mornings on Crocker Springs,
Floyd up early across the road, hoeing his garden,
careful around corn roots and crook-necked squash—

slow and deliberate his every move, less a rhythm
than a study. Floyd taught by saying what not to do—
"Too much clay in this soil to plant wet," he said.

But I planted, and the surface dried into concrete
sprouts couldn't break. Splitting wood, I buried
a wedge in a bodock knot. Spent half the morning

hacking the log, until Floyd crossed the road,
said I might burn it free. I was teaching out of state
when my wife called about his stroke—laid all day

on his trailer floor until his grandson found him.
Driving home from Virginia to Tennessee, I saw
his stance in every garden, his pause at the block

of every farmer splitting wood. When I moved
to Crocker Springs, I started writing daily about
growing up in a town next to the Mississippi.

Awake at five, I learned how light claims an orchard.
I banged an old Underwood and sometimes my head
against the study wall. Frustrated, I'd walk the hill

in early spring and count the woodstoves down the hollow,
searching for a boy I buried when my father died,
burning and burning him free.

Driving Ridge Road, Writing this Poem

A cool drizzle, early September, ground fog
covers the stubble of fresh cut hay.
Rumor has it that an old man who

is learning to love his life drives Ridge Road,
writing poems on his steering wheel.
Each letter zigs when he shifts gears,

so that g's look like s's. The seed okra
grows as big as rockets, but no red flares
disrupt this morning of ordinary miracles.

You must pay attention or you'll miss
the red-tail perched on the church steeple,
or the humped shoulders of buzzards

performing an autopsy on a dead doe.
If you drive too close, they hop like kangaroos,
their wings lifting like the arms of old men

in water aerobics. Cow pasture gives way
to woods lined with blue ageratum, goldenrod,
ironweed and late summer asters.

Then an open meadow, mature grass-seed ashimmer
with purple subtle enough to break a painter's heart.
I shift down to third and think of Rumi, world

and time away, dancing creation, of Blake,
in his backyard conversing with God,
of Mary Oliver, who spying mockingbirds

in a territorial spin, saw the awesome gods
revealing themselves to the humble couple
willing to share their meager meal.

Overwhelmed, an old fart like me, writing a poem
on his steering wheel, sees Baby Girl and Dakota,
his neighbor's adopted mustangs, swanning around

at the fence, remembers James Wright,
and suddenly realizes that if he brakes,
shifts into second, he might blossom.

Whisper

In small town Tennessee,
my brother, Clark, drinks coffee
at the kitchen table and converses
with Lizzy, the chocolate lab.
They ride together to Sandi's farm
to give sweet mix to the horses,
then walk the fence line counting cows.
Clark will think about our grandfather
at Bible Hill. Which story will he tell
himself today? Perhaps the morning
the mare, Nell, birthed a jack.
Grandmilt rolled his white shirt sleeve
up to his arm pit, and the mare let him
reach through her birth canal to make sure
all was clear. Then he dug the hard turds
from the foal's anus with fingers,
releasing the bowel fluid that would
assure the little mule would live.
Clark's eyes well up, and he grieves
for Grandmilt and our father,
grieves for the years themselves
that number down so quickly.
He laughs at himself, whistles for Lizzy,
out of sight chasing squirrels.
He will work all day, relish the smell
of hay and his own sweat that collects
dust in creases on his neck.
Other stories will come—
the night the mussel fisherman
drove up River Road with one arm
to get Grandmilt to remove a barbed hook
from his palm, or one of many nights
the little house was knocked awake
to help a neighbor pull a calf

or draw the fever from a child.
There are more stories than afternoon can hold.
Clark will quit at dusk, wash at the watering trough
and stop by the VFW for a whiskey.
Lizzy will be there fussing at his side.
After supper, he will close the night
like the day was opened, conversing
with the chocolate lab at the kitchen table.
They might clean a shotgun, oil a pair
of boots, and pray for his children,
grandchildren, and Beverly, his first love
who died in a house fire. He will take
a glass of red wine to the porch
and listen to darkness whisper the years.

Autumn Thoughts

Sunday free, I drive Ridge Road, watch vultures circle.
Starlings in amazing precision scour a field,
give the illusion of dark waves. Seedpods hang
from leafless mimosas. Moss carpeting stone outcrops
gives the winter forest its only green. In late November,
the spirit, fat from autumn, is ready to hibernate.
It welcomes the small beauties—the figured leaves
of pipsissewa, white bell-shaped flowers turned
to gray beads ripe for spring. The dance slows
but never stops. Days like this I think of my sister.
In early winter, the leaves raked and burned,
we sat at her piano singing show tunes—
Carnival, Oklahoma, South Pacific, The Fantastics.
Sometimes we left the bench and blocked a scene,
bellowing *Who can I be, now that I can't be me anymore,*
until Josephus, our spaniel, howled along.
Ours was a musical home—our brother's bebop,
father singing *I'll fly away* in the shower,
my mother humming '40s love songs in the kitchen
with a voice that would offend a crow. Memory serves
as a kind of prayer—how a hardwood forest flavored
with a spot of moss brings *Try to Remember* on the tongue,
There Ain't Nothing like a Dame, Bring in the Clowns—
how a heaviness comes and goes with memory—
a brother's bowie knife, a father's funeral,
a student's suicide, a girl's face, her name forgotten,
a picture of an army buddy who died in Vietnam
found in a jacket I couldn't throw away.

V

Waking

Waking

I wake each morning and read the window for weather,
as drops of condensation run down the pane
like mist on magnolia. Soft morning illuminates
the bedroom, and even early birds mute their songs.

How slow time wakes when work is forgotten,
and obligations drift out the kitchen window
like the scent of coffee. September has come and gone
with little to say except everything that lives past summer

doesn't die. October isn't a preface to winter,
but a sky-blue month when rain turns cold,
clouds float high and lonely, and our little star makes
broken shadows of leaves drifting across the river.

Today a kingfisher rattles his journey through the valley,
and two crows preen first light into morning.
This is how I learn to say my name again, since waking
isn't a metaphor, and time means more than money.

The Appointment

It's hard to start every day anew,
the mind ragtag with sleep's phantoms

and daily habits as unavoidable
as cat litter. Why not be late for

your 9 o'clock with the committee?
Tell them you're sorry, but you stopped

to chaperone a tortoise crossing a road.
Tell them you couldn't ignore

the harbingers of spring—bloodroot,
hepatica, wild iris. Tell them tribal peoples

used bloodroot as an aphrodisiac,
spread blood-red dye on their faces.

Tell them Greeks used hepatica to heal
the liver, that an iris held to a cheek

feels as waxy sweet as a girl's ear.
Tell them that while mulching the garden

you found a ringneck snake, most private
of animals, its tiny necklace yellow

with new scales. Tell them that you
wish to renegotiate your travel plans,

extend your all-too-brief visit to this planet,
that you need time off to file your nails

so when you make love to your wife
you won't harm her perfect skin.

Thespian

Shall I believe that unsubstantial Death is amorous…
—Shakespeare's *Romeo*

My cat pokes a hognose snake in the yard.
The snake plays dead, the opossum
of the serpent world—rolls on its back,
exposes its belly scales, writhes,

twists a grotesque mouth, sticks
out its tongue. The cat gets bored,
but I'm not. This tragedienne could
play Juliet. I lift the snake by the tail,

lay it in thick grass, and stand back.
When it feels safe, it cracks an eye,
turns on its stomach and skedaddles.
My herpetology friends would claim this

death-feign a function of natural selection,
shaped and perfected over millions of years,
like goats that faint, and marsupials
that play dead in my garbage can.

I admire the majesty of creation,
but want to know which ancient
hognose snake first performed
the act of dying to save its own skin.

Alas, some things I'll never know.
Having lost a brace of kinsmen,
Escalus scorns the feuding families,
and *all are punish'd;* the curtain falls

and the dead actors arise: Mercutio,
Tybalt, Paris, Romeo and Juliet, wash off
their makeup and head to the Dirty Duck
for a pint with fish and chips.

As for you, little thespian, be off
to gorge on lizards, mice, and insects,
knowing that, like the fairest youth
of Verona, you have died to live another day.

The Names of Creeks

—for James Still

Today the rounds of hay sit quietly in their fields.
A light frost melts from their tops, steams the air
like loaves of fresh bread on someone's porch.

The hills, like the heads of children sleeping,
are scruffed with hardwoods. They tangle
with huckleberry, like my morning heart,

not easy to sort through, pathless and mum.
Accept whatever comes a great poet said. I want
to invert that thought: come to whatever accepts,

but the words don't make the right sense exactly.
Today sense nestles in the names of creeks:
Dry Fork, Crippled, Troublesome, New Hope.

May Morning, Reelfoot Lake

Morning studies the edge of the lake
                                like a heron,
seems to pause   just before a wren calls,
easing the tension.
                    You say a word in your sleep
like a greeting,   turn over
                              wrapping your head in the sheet.
I don't know why our lives
                      unfold like a story
or the lake can't be separated
                      from morning.
Soon you will sit up and ask for coffee
                              then check
the bookmark to make sure
                      the novel didn't
read without you.
An osprey cries—I turn to watch it alight
                                  on a cypress snag—
its wings mock-flying   which is its custom.
Your head emerges from the sheet
                            and I rise to pour coffee,
two sugars and cream.
A heron lifts from lily pads
                      and begins its journey,
dragging shadows west
                to the river.

Siasconset Time

—after Eavan Boland

Time is measured by the pace of waves;
skate eggs, whelk chains, and seaweed
mark high tide. She reads Tao on the sand,
presses primrose and yellow scotch broom,

while he casts for blues off the point.
Later, darkness hides an inch of wine
left in a glass, her hair against his cheek,
footprints snaking tide and sand along the beach.

Words get lost on islands; what was meant,
remembered best by lips, restful sleep,
the tips of fingers. In the morning, fog hides
the house, the hamlet, all but the ocean's roar.

Back in the city, he recalls the endless swells
stretching a dark sea larger than a continent.
She dreams a bright line sweeping across the shore,
the surprise of roses when the fog lifts.

Early this Morning

The sheet pulled away
and your scar glowed
like a crescent moon
in the quiet light.
My first impulse
was to cover you
but found myself studying
how flesh and skin heal,
how tiny tracks disappear
to form a symbol
like primitive cave paintings:
a bone tool like a scythe,
the rounded slope of elk.
What would an anthropologist
say about this tiny icon;
that it signifies genetic curse,
something sinister in our world
that spirits female cells awry?

Does it stand for survival, shame,
bravery, fear, as you sit in
a warm tub examining
your own tissue, searching
for the smallest lump?
You stir and I tuck the sheet
around your shoulder, careful
to cover this pale halo
in the safety of our room.
How will you tell me
if there is a next time:
over coffee, in the car
on the way to work?
When is there a right
moment, though we have
slept three decades
skin to skin?

On a Trail Near Shining Rock

If someday we were walking a trail,
tunneled with laurel, and columbine
rose up from the ankles of rhododendron,
and I turned to see if you had noticed,
and found that you weren't with me,
a darkness would settle over my shoulders.

My mind practices such sorrow
as I take your hand to guide around
a sharp snag before the trail turns steep.
All morning we have stared down
at trip roots and rocks to keep from falling.
We stop to view layered mountains
when a break in foliage opens the horizon.

In the Sawtooth Mountains of Idaho
we couldn't escape the big blue.
Even deep in a canyon, a kaleidoscope
of light brushed stone and pine with sky.
High desert makes one feel insignificant.
But in Appalachia near Shinning Rock,
a green tunnel of flora opening
to a sudden view moves the mind
toward mirror, toward shadow.

We stand together, sun warming our faces.
A layer of clouds blankets East Fork.
Every trickle, rivulet and cascade flows
toward the French Broad watershed,
buried beneath canopy. Our fingertips
brush slightly, just enough to feel
the dry, honest sense of touch
before starting the last leg to the falls.

Lifting

The way my father lifted me
to retrieve the key from the doorframe
of the old lake cabin is how
I've always imagined being lifted
again in some hour, lifted up, up,

feeling, not blindly, but with the eyes of my
fingers, for something that abides in darkness.
But the old skeleton key with the fog patina,
accompanied by an acrid dust of oak
and a few ragged spider eggs was enough.

We uncovered chairs and fake leather couch,
swept dead wasps from the kitchen floor,
and as I carried gear from the trunk,
he pumped water for coffee and lit the stove.
I sipped it black, watched the muscles

in my father's cheeks and forehead relax,
and wondered if learning to sip scalding coffee,
the bitterness breaking through the sugar,
was one of the secrets of being a man.
We ate sandwiches my mother had packed,

and he said that he would teach me how
to listen. As the moon rose and dragged its
tail across the lake, a chorus of frogs
and owls crowded the early June night,
and he named them all and I suspect

made up a few. This would be the only
night my father and I spent alone,
away from my brothers, sister
and mother; the only night away
from scout troops of men and boys.

That night as I watched my father doze,
a smile returned to his face, and a pride
of sharing his knowing beyond the daily
grease of car engines and complaints.
I still feel the ease with which he lifted me,

age nine, with the assurance that
I would find the key, the one with
the fog patina, caught in the fog
of memory—of something almost lost
and perhaps found in darkness.

Cold Comfort

Lying in bed, winter dreams
like a wrinkled pillow
mark his face. He breathes
in the cold upstairs of the house
and pictures a cord of oak
split and stacked beside the porch.
Muscles in his shoulders ache,
the small of his back tender
with turning. An emptiness
fills the window where bits
of sleet bounce like beads
of water in a hot skillet.
The boy in him welcomes
winter's first storm. The man
charts the odds, what toll
it will take on the house,
the trees, the neighbor's horses,
old lady Sutton down the road
who gimps to the mailbox
on one crutch.

No clear sky coyote calls
to tune up farm dogs,
just a banging bird feeder
with a raccoon riding it
like a trapeze. Every living thing
that isn't starving seeks shelter.
Loneliness comes with the thought
of his father: blindness in his open eyes,
the self gone from his face.
A week before his death,
his ungloved hands were never cold.
He'd warm children's cheeks
with callused fingers. Sometimes

a January storm measures the heart.
Why the sound of night sleet
summons the dead has no answer,
just the pang of memory
and its comfort.

Midnight Mass

I wax floors the way my father taught me,
on my knees with a rag and Johnson's paste,
putting my shoulder into it, rubbing
half moons of dull wax with each swirl.

From my knees my room is a sanctuary
and monotonous labor a prayer. It's good
to be tired my father said; a tired man
can rest even when he can't sleep. So

while everyone's in bed on our country road,
I'm holding church and conjuring spirits
with my ragged Ouija: mother's girlhood
picture on the wall, grandfather's

steamboat chest in the corner, a rifle,
my sixteenth birthday present, clean
and silent for thirty years, a computer,
my second memory, looks out of place

on the antique desk. I light a candle
and feel my father in the reflected
motion of my labor rising up from
the floor into my shoulder.

Pruning

When you dreamed yourself
back in the farm house
beside the orchard, it wasn't
the spring breeze you remembered,

but hours of pruning. Your father
said to open the center of each tree
to light. Avoid rust by cutting limbs
that rub the wind together,

destroy suckers that rise from roots.
Cut without mercy to bring
the good fruit. One night after
a week of pruning, you awoke

with sore shoulders and hands
to look out the window and see branches
of apple and pear catch the moon
the length of their trunks. Stark limbs

reached out like stick men
in children's drawings. You feared
that if you trimmed your life as bare,
the music you heard inside

would sound as trite as a TV jingle,
the high lonesome of your father's
work song might leave your blood.
Don't despair. The song's pulse

needs repetition and simple words
to catch life's cadence. Your dream
can't solve the heart's longing,
but pruning awakens it to light.

Alchemy

—for Peter Stillman

I often think I hear your voice
skimming a wave like a least tern,
not the sound but the shimmer,

and how the tern rises,
then spears the ocean is how
a thought occurs to you—that sudden,

with a smile, other times a frown.
A dark shadow must be severed
from your lung. I think of the worn

burl pipe I sent, how you kept it filled,
a ponderous scent I loved.
I am dazzled still by your poetry—

how a startle of pigeon wings in the barn
becomes a lover's breath, how a wife's
bow stroke in a canoe is a sacrament

as holy as oxygen, how a winter afternoon
in the Catskills dissolves as surely
as a gray horse in snow.

I hold your book this morning
and remember the turn of a curve
in Idaho that opened a mountain range

covered in frost. I'm not sure where
this poem is leading—a high desert
pass white with sego lilies, or a river

where cliff swallows chase an osprey,
or offshore a tern spears the ocean,
and light on water is the sound of our voices.

Driving Country Roads on Sunday

Sometimes the silhouette of a crow appears
in an oak snag instead of a cross on Decoration Day.

There's nothing more certain than the grief
of leaving grass hills for an eternity elsewhere.

Ear lobe of a girl, owl talon, newt spot,
divided, separated, unfolded, born: all with

a memory like tree roots dying to be reshaped.
Is this enough or doesn't the heart design its

own fate and practice believing it. These aren't
new questions, just a terrible dilemma, half home-

sickness, half hope. It doesn't matter about whose
version of the truth, only the lies we tell ourselves

to believe. At the Freewill Baptist Church,
the parking lot is filled with cars of the faithful.

A blue heron wades Jackman Creek. Around
the corner a startling sight, a marsh hawk atop

a dead doe ripping a torn gut. Beside Branch Shoals,
stark arms of sycamore reach toward a January sky

where wood ducks fly just short of heaven.

The Prayerful Agnostic

He is thankful for food and shelter,
for books and music, for trees, birds,
and flowers. He bows his head before sleeping

and lets the wind outside his window whisper,
lets creation nestled in molecules and stars
continue its patient journey. Purpose

is a concept he considers, beyond the nudge
of DNA, beyond the urgent call of glands.
In his fifties, lust hasn't disappeared,

But a different surge, more dangerous
haunts his blood: the hollow thought
of nothing. Some addictions are closely

linked to what one cannot feel, to where
one dare not go. The lure away from sorrow
and expectation, the magnet that is darkness.

In mid-January, the tulip bulbs peer through
his garden. Tonight a hard freeze burns
sprouts back into their little tombs.

The prayerful agnostic will blanket
each with mulch. He can't bear
the thought of spring without them.

Apologies

I want to apologize
for the sun today,
the way it filters winter trees
to warm the porch,
for its refusal to acknowledge
the clouds on the horizon,
or the shadows that grow
as afternoon walks its
slow walk toward night.

Darkness collects
in the center of rocks,
in the hollows
of dying sycamores,
in the eyes of the dead doe
that weave a circle
of buzzards above
our country road.

But the sun knows night
can't hide the hulking barn,
the sifting sound that grass
makes in the breeze,
the silence of animals
who use the night to feed,
the stars that flutter
between a skeleton of limbs,
the crucial work of rhizomes
humming beneath the ground.

And what do we make at night
that's nearly as important,
a heartbreak of to-dos that keep
us living in the future,

a rumination of concerns
that interrupts slumber? Where
enters grace in such a life?
So I apologize for my apology.
The sun keeps its appointments
without worry. The doe, barn,
and sycamore will crumble
into a memory of stars.
The grasses and irises
will continue to plan
until a crucible silences
their cold burning, long
before our sun says goodnight.

August Moon

Late August,
    a gentle rain all morning,
a stillness of drops
     coats maple leaves,
paints the brick walk
     a red sheen.
In the night, a Luna moth tattooed
      the barn-wood door.
I light a candle on the porch,
    water the jade and bamboo.
The purple ironweed
    Suzanne gathered in the field
fades brown,
    and little daisies hang
from a bucket like dead spiders.

Windy days
    announce change,
but quiet days open a different self
    that waits for another
bird to visit the feeder,
    a beetle to bang the screen.

    As the candle burns down,
a haunting
    invades, as it will,
from a thicket of birdcalls, lost places,
    missing faces
like those in windows of passing cars.
    A breeze picks up,
and the moth flies away
    leaving the barn-wood
moonless.

Druid Thoughts in November

Driving alone down Baker Station Road,
I find myself in love again with the hills

that form Highland Rim. Late November
and the skeletal scruff of hardwoods,

the bright colors gone, only a scatter
of brown leaves tag beech and oak,

stubborn centenarians reluctant to let go—
unlike maple and gum that turn endearingly

beautiful, then give leaves up to the forest loam.
Both qualities admirable in human terms,

but no hidden message here, just observations
from a person among trees. I'm not envious

of a life lived two hundred years, rooted
with outstretched limbs as earth tilts the seasons.

But I might abide for a time, shading
stone outcrops and creeks, watching

forest creatures go about their journeys
as owls haunt the shadows with muted voices.

I am not Thoreau or Merlin who understood
the songs of wind in trees. Call it what you will,

all humans buy and sell to live, but there are those
who may not know that a possession is not

as grand as an oak, no habit as comely
as sycamore bark, no hieroglyph like

dark limbs to mark a winter heart.

Journey

> *I have traveled widely in Concord.*
> —Thoreau

Through the leaf-strewn yard of autumn—
oak, hickory and sweet gum, maple and persimmon—
I hear roughly the same hush under boot,

and the snap of dry twigs. Because my home
is on the ridge top, I drive through the hills
that follow Sulfur Fork, greet turkey and deer,

speak kindly to the old black lab
who sleeps in the road by her barn.
I've stopped to watch a kestrel, copper

and gray sentinel, scour a field for mice.
I've read the pecking order of buzzards
feeding on a doe's belly, studied how

they tear the rich viscera, then hop
and squawk with a relish of joy.
I've seen children tour an ancient cemetery,

reading epitaphs and names. I've studied
grave diggers, shoulder deep in soil,
shoring up a shadowed grave as an egret

fished a hilltop pond, as dusk drown
the sun in a scurry of mauve. Follow
the sycamore leaf's downward spiral

and learn of the heart's meter,
that in an average life it echoes
two and a half billion beats. How long

I failed to heed what childhood taught me—
the slowing of the pulse as night comes on,
the sound of the earth beneath my feet.

The Graciousness of Soil

—after Malena Morling

In refugee camps, my mother
would have cleaned the matted
hair of children, sheltered infants
and taught the unschooled how
to read, the way she did on her

small town street in Tennessee.
In the endless parade of families
crossing war-torn borders,
she would have cooked and fed,
the way she did for homeless men

traveling down Old Highway 51.
Before the mumble of old age,
she died rereading Thoreau,
who said in close observation
one owns all that one surveys.

So in death my mother carried
with her the loneliness of a husband
sent to war, the loss of a sister
and infant during childbirth. In death
she cherished the whistle of finches,

the cricket whispers of waxwings,
the shameless antics of egrets
in their mating. In death she knew
the heaviness of being human,
perhaps lifted, perhaps not. In

the tatted doily of Queen Anne's lace,
in the veined leaf of pipsissewa,
in the honey musk of persimmon,
in the flap-eared petal of poppy,
a calmness waits, then recedes into

seed and soil, she said, and begins
again. This is how my brothers
and sister thought of eternity,
the sorrow only human, and even
if some dimension of Heaven kept

our spirits (which my mother believed
was true), the homesickness would
abide for having lived on earth.
In her prayers dogs were included,
especially Wags, the wayward spaniel.

In her prayers, world suffering
was not lifted, nor accepted,
the heaviness of being human,
a poppy losing its petals to
the gracious, ever patient soil.

Indigo

The light which dwells in our words
—Jeff Hardin

One can hear the river in a poem,
feel the tug of forever as the moon
glints the shoals, the current constant,
the light changing interpretation as
the planet moves. The light on a bunting's

wing becomes the word bunting
and will always be that light, half
bluebird, half sun god. Indico, from
Spanish, from Latin, indicum, from
Greek, indikon, "Indian (dye)," from Indikos.

How far can you trace a color in language,
the same timeless sun bouncing off
feathers as they flutter across the road.
The word, "mother" (she who first
pointed out the bird feeding in river grass)

will always be part of that name,
her face visiting dreams years after
her death. So say the word "bunting"
and indigo will follow and the memory
of the one who taught this bird

at the edge of the river where the sun
still bounces off a roll of shoals, where
a person might come to reclaim a part
of the self, in hopes that the light which
dwells in words in some way dwells in us.

Coda

Solstice

To learn about light
I sit on the porch and watch
winter trees filter sun.

I never know how to greet silence,
except to breathe quietly, monitor
heart thumps in my temples.

This morning blood and sun
are part of the mystery
alchemists ignored.

The hawk in its lonely circle knows.
The crow tells its shadow.
I'm taking notes on milkweed,

how the pods creep open
and loose angels into light.
Monarch butterflies feed

on those toxic plants,
teach birds not to eat
bright wings. Everything

sublime isn't deadly
and that's another season.
Today is early December.

The sky, a deeper blue, floats
toward the longest night
when the pulse slows,

when light is more need
than blessing, when things
that glitter are almost gold.

Colophon

Bembo was modeled on typefaces cut by Francesco Griffo for Aldus Manutius' printing of *De Aetna* in 1495 in Venice, a book by classicist Pietro Bembo about his visit to Mount Etna. Griffo's design is considered one of the first of the old style typefaces, which include Garamond, that were used as staple text types in Europe for 200 years. Stanley Morison supervised the design of Bembo for the Monotype Corporation in 1929. Bembo is a fine text face because of its well-proportioned letterforms, functional serifs, and lack of peculiarities; the italic is modeled on the handwriting of the Renaissance scribe Giovanni Tagliente. Books and other texts set in Bembo can encompass a large variety of subjects and formats because of its quiet classical beauty and its high readability.

The cover photograph, "Cypress Reflections on a Foggy Morning," was taken at Reelfoot Lake by Tina Marie Brookes of Nashville, Tennessee. This photograph won Second Place in the Brentwood Camera Club Open Photo of the Month in September, 2008. For more information visit her website: www.tinamariebrookes.com.

Bill Brown is the author of three chapbooks, four collections of poetry and a writing textbook on which he collaborated with Malcolm Glass. His most recent titles are *Late Winter* (IRIS PRESS, 2008) and *Tatters* (MARCH STREET PRESS, 2007). During the past twenty years, he has published hundreds of poems and articles in journals, magazines and anthologies. In 1999 Brown wrote and co-produced the Instructional Television Series, *Student Centered Learning*, for Nashville Public Television. He holds a degree in history from Bethel College and graduate degrees in English from the Bread Loaf School of English, Middlebury College and George Peabody College. For twenty years, Brown directed an award winning writing program at an academic magnet school in Nashville. He retired in 2003 and accepted a part-time lecturer position at Vanderbilt University. In 1995 the National Foundation for Advancement in the Arts named him Distinguished Teacher in the Arts. He has been a Scholar in Poetry at the Bread Loaf Writers Conference, a Fellow at the Virginia Center for the Creative Arts, and a two-time recipient of Fellowships in poetry from the Tennessee Arts Commission. He and his wife Suzanne live in the hills north of Nashville with a tribe of cats.

www.ingramcontent.com/pod-product-compliance
Lightning Source LLC
Chambersburg PA
CBHW022134080426
42734CB00006B/354